Read

Urdu script

Read and write Urdu script

Richard Delacy

For UK order enquiries: please contact Bookpoint Ltd, 130 Milton Park, Abingdon, Oxon OX14 4SB. Telephone: +44 (0) 1235 827720. Fax: +44 (0) 1235 400454. Lines are open 09.00–17.00, Monday to Saturday, with a 24-hour message answering service. Details about our titles and how to order are available at www.teachyourself.com

For USA order enquiries: please contact
McGraw-Hill Customer Services,
PO Box 545, Blacklick, OH 43004-0545, USA.
Telephone: 1-800-722-4726. Fax: 1-614-755-5645.

For Canada order enquiries: please contact
McGraw-Hill Ryerson Ltd,
300 Water St, Whitby, Ontario L1N 9B6, Canada.
Telephone: 905 430 5000. Fax: 905 430 5020.

Long renowned as the authoritative source for self-guided learning – with more than 50 million copies sold worldwide – the **Teach Yourself** series includes over 500 titles in the fields of languages, crafts, hobbies, business, computing and education.

British Library Cataloguing in Publication Data: a catalogue record for this title is available from the British Library.

Library of Congress Catalog Card Number: on file.

First published in UK 2001 as *Teach Yourself Beginner's Urdu Script* by Hodder Education, part of Hachette UK, 338 Euston Road, London NW1 3BH.

First published in US 2001 by The McGraw-Hill Companies, Inc.

This edition published 2010.

Typeset by MPS Limited, A Macmillan Company.

Printed in Great Britain for Hodder Education, an Hachette UK Company, 338 Euston Road, London NW1 3BH.

Impression number 10 9 8 7

Year 2016

Contents

Abbreviation

(m) or (f) after a noun indicates that it is respectively masculine or feminine.

Meet the author

I initially studied Hindi for three years at college in Australia, after which I spent a year in New Delhi undertaking further studies at the Central Hindi Institute. I returned to Australia and commenced teaching Hindi at the college level, at which time I also began my study of Urdu. I completed an MA in History, before embarking on higher studies in the United States. While in America I have taught Hindi and Urdu at the University of Chicago, the University of Illinois at Chicago and Harvard University. I am the co-author of *Elementary Hindi* and *Elementary Hindi Workbook* (Tuttle Publishing, 2009) and authored the Hindi-Urdu section of the *Hindi, Urdu and Bengali: Lonely Planet Phrasebook* (Lonely Planet Publishers, 2005). I currently live in Cambridge, Massachusetts, and I travel back to India frequently.

Richard Delacy

Only got a minute?

Having evolved in north India, Urdu is the national language of Pakistan as well as one of the main languages of India. It is conventionally written in a script called **Nasta'līq**, which literally means 'the hanging **Naskh**', **Naskh** being the script most commonly used to write the Arabic language. The **Nasta'līq** script is also used to write several other languages in Pakistan and India, including Kashmiri and Panjabi (in Pakistan). The same script was also formerly employed to write Persian but Persian is now conventionally written in the **Naskh** script. The principal difference between the **Naskh** and **Nasta'līq** scripts is that words in the **Naskh** script run along a line, whereas words in the **Nasta'līq** slant diagonally.

السّلام علیکم	السّلام عليكم
Nasta'līq	**Naskh**

In addition to being the national language of Pakistan, Urdu possesses a rich literary tradition, both in prose and in poetry, dating back to at least the beginning of the eighteenth century. Learning to read the script is the first step on the way to enjoying this long and rich tradition as well as developing the necessary skills to read, write and speak modern Urdu.

The **Nasta'līq** script is cursive and runs from right to left. There are thirty-five characters, each of which has a name in addition to its pronunciation. Most of the characters are made up of a linear portion together with dots, or in the case of three characters a symbol that resembles a small 'flat' symbol in music. Most, but not all, of the characters connect to both the preceding and following character. There are four characters that do not connect to the following character. Coincidentally, they happen to be the four characters that make up the word 'Urdu'.

و	دُ	ر	اُ
ū	**d**	**r**	**u**

(vāo) (dāl) (re) (alif)

Whatever your reason for learning Urdu, this introduction to the script will provide you with the best possible foundation to begin reading and writing **Nasta'līq** fluently, the first step in the journey to learning the language proper.

5 Only got five minutes?

The Nasta'līq script, which contains 35 characters, is a modified form of the Arabic script. The Arabic script was first modified and employed to write Persian and then further modified to represent what came to be known as the Urdu language as it evolved in north India over the course of the 18th century. This modification took the form of the addition of several characters (modified forms of existing characters) to represent sounds that do not occur in Arabic. How this modified form of the Arabic script came to be employed to write languages in the subcontinent, a long distance from where the script originated, is related to Muslim influence in South Asia from around the 13th century onwards. Both Arabic and Persian were important languages for Muslims who settled in India and eventually came to rule much of the subcontinent between the 14th and 19th centuries. During this time, Arabic remained important as the language of the Holy Quran and traditional learning, and Persian remained an important spoken language, a language of learning, as well as the language of the bureaucracy, at least until the early nineteenth century. These languages also came to influence the spoken languages that were evolving in and around Delhi in particular, mainly in the form of the incorporation of many words of Persian and Arabic origin. Eventually the language that evolved in urban centers in the north came to be written by educated elites in this modified form of the Arabic script. Over time, the pronunciation of many words that contained distinctly Arabic and Persian sounds was diluted by many speakers who came to adopt these words into their lexicon. The spellings of these words have, however, largely remained faithful to the original Persian and Arabic spellings, even if many speakers do not differentiate between these sounds and other sounds that already existed in local languages.

Apart from its significance as a modern spoken language in India and Pakistan, Urdu is also a language with a considerably rich literary tradition that dates back at least until the beginning of the eighteenth century. It is considered a very poetic language, primarily because much of this literary tradition consists of poetry composed by nobles and patronized poets both in the South of India and in the major centers of Muslim rule in the north: Delhi and Lucknow. From its beginnings as the script used to compose poetry, this modified form of the Arabic script gradually came to be employed more widely for this evolving urban language spoken in the north of India. With the evolution of prose literature in the nineteenth century, Urdu became an important vehicle for modern literature as well, especially over the course of the twentieth century. This has continued, primarily in the genre of the short story, until the present day. Commercial films produced in Bombay also still contain a considerable lexicon that is drawn from Persian and Arabic, particularly in the lyrics of many songs. This is due in part to the fact that love songs in particular have traditionally drawn heavily from images and vocabulary of earlier Urdu poetry.

Nasta'līq is a cursive script. Most, but not all, of the characters in **Nasta'līq** connect to both the preceding and the following character. This means that characters that connect on both sides have four forms, depending on the position they occupy in a word. That is to say, they have an initial form, a medial form, a final form and an independent form. Take a look at the second character of the alphabet, which is called **be** and represents the consonant **b**.

ب

be (b)

ـب	ـبـ	بـ	ب
final form	medial form	initial form	independent form

Characters that only connect to the preceding character have only two forms (an independent/initial form and a medial/final form).

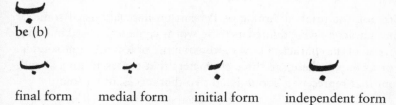

There are ten vowels in Urdu: three short vowels and seven long vowels. The three short vowels, **a** (as in 'ago'), **i** (as in 'hit'), and **u** (as in 'put') are **not** represented by characters in the script. The other seven long vowels are represented by only three of the characters. To help identify when one of the three short vowels is to be pronounced, there exist three small symbols that may be employed. In the same way that the characters have names, these small symbols also have names. Two of them are written above characters and one is written below characters.

َ zabar (written above the character) = **a**
ِ zer (written below the character) = **i**
ُ pesh (written above the character) = **u**

While these symbols are employed in dictionaries and introductory books like this one, ordinarily they are not used other than to avoid confusion in handwritten or printed texts.

The first character in the alphabet is the character **alif** ا. It is a non-connector (does not join to the following character). When it occurs at the beginning of a word, it is used to represent one of the three short vowels described above. Take a look at the combination of **alif** with **be** below.

اُب	اِب	اَب
ub	**ib**	**ab**

Because the original Arabic or Persian pronunciations of some of the characters were diluted as these words came to be used in Urdu, several of the characters now represent more or less the same sounds. For example, there are three characters that represent an **s** sound, four that represent a **z** sound and two that represent a **t** sound.

ص ث س	**s**
ظ ض ذ ز	**z**
ط ت	**t**

This means that spelling in Urdu can be a little more challenging and the forms of entire words should be learnt rather than literally spelling them out character by character. Over time it becomes easier to anticipate which characters will occur, in particular as you become more familiar with words of Arabic and Persian origin in the language. One of the chief benefits of this book over other Urdu script books is that there is hardly a piece of writing introduced in the script that is not a real word. The reason for this is that the learner must recognize and be able to pronounce whole words as quickly as possible. As far as possible, words are introduced in this book in a manner that enables the student to learn a core vocabulary of common everyday words before going on to study the language. Words are also introduced initially with vowel markers to indicate where short vowels are to be pronounced and then later repeated without these vowel makers so that the student may learn to recognize them as they would appear in real texts. There are also systematic diagrams to assist in the production of the characters in the various forms they take in the different positions in a word.

The Urdu language is both poetically beautiful as well as possessing one of the most ornate and beautiful scripts of any language. With the right introduction, this script is easy to learn to read and very enjoyable to write. Whether you want to read Urdu poetry, understand the lyrics of many Bollywood film songs or learn to speak modern Urdu, *Read and write Urdu script* is the first step along the way to enjoying all that this language has to offer.

10 Only got ten minutes?

The script that is used to write Urdu, **Nasta'līq**, is more or less the same as the script that is used to write Arabic, **Naskh**. Literally **Nasta'līq** means 'the hanging **Naskh**' and words in **Nasta'līq** appear to hang and slant diagonally, whereas words in **Naskh** run along an imaginary bottom line. This script was also used to write Persian until the 20th century when, with the advent of printing in what is now modern-day Iran, a shift to **Naskh** took place. The central importance of Persian written in **Nasta'līq** in the arts and statecraft from the sixteenth century in South Asia meant that this ornate form of script maintained its prominence in India until the evolution of Urdu in the nineteenth century. For a number of reasons, one of which was a highly developed calligraphic tradition, most Urdu texts continued to be produced in **Nasta'līq** in India even after the advent of printing technologies. This does not mean that **Naskh** is never employed for Urdu texts in India and Pakistan, but even today there remains a preference for the more ornate **Nasta'līq** script. With the development of **Nasta'līq** fonts for computer software programs, **Nasta'līq** continues to be the first choice for the production of the majority of texts in the Urdu language.

Whereas in **Naskh** there are really only two forms of characters (an initial/medial form and an independent form), because of the ornate, more cursive nature of **Nasta'līq**, there are four forms of characters that connect to both the preceding character and the following character. Those characters that do not connect to the following character possess only two forms (and initial/independent form and a medial/final form).

Let's take a look at the following two characters and how they are combined to create words.

	final	medial	initial	independent
be (b)	ـب	ـبـ	بـ	ب

kāf (k) ـک ـکـ کـ ک

We can take the initial form of **be** and combine it with the final form of **kāf** thus:

بک ـک ـک بـ

bak (*nonsense*, f)

This could also be pronounced as:

بِک بُک

bik (stem of the verb *to be sold*) or **buk** (the English word *book*)

We can clarify which of the three short vowels (see above) should be pronounced with these characters by using the small symbols introduced earlier. For example:

بک بِک بُک

bak **bik** **buk**

To simplify things, in this book only the symbols indicating short **i** and short **u** vowels are employed. If there is no symbol, you should assume that the vowel is a short **a** vowel. Remember that none of these three short vowels can appear at the end of a word. If there is a consonant in a word final position, you should assume that no vowel is pronounced with it.

For example:

بک بِک بُک

bak **bik** **buk**

Similarly, we can take the initial form of **kāf** and combine it with the final form of **be** in the following manner:

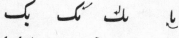

final	medial	initial	independent
ـب	ـبـ	بـ	ب
ـک	ـکـ	کـ	ک

کب

kab (*when*)

Let's take a look at a longer word. Using the same two characters, we can combine the initial form of **be** with the medial form of **kāf**, add the medial form of **be** and the final form of **kāf** to make another common word.

بکبک

bakbak (*nonsense*, f)

While you might expect this word to be pronounced as **bakabak**, because it is actually made up of the word **bak** repeated, there is no vowel sound pronounced after the first **k** in the middle of the word.

Let's take a closer look at how we form these words.

bak

kab

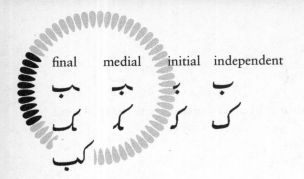

bakbak

Now let's add another two characters so that we can make a few more words. The first of these is the character that represents an l sound, **lām**. It connects to both the preceding and following characters in a word.

	final	medial	initial	independent
lām (l)	ـل	ـلـ	لـ	ل

We can take the initial form of **lām** and add it to the final form of **be** thus:

لب   لـ ـب   لـ

lab (*lip*, m)

We can also take the initial form of **be** and join it to the final form of **lām** thus:

بل   بـ ـل   بـ

bal (*strength*, *force*, m)

Now we can add the character **alif** to these characters. **Alif** is the first character in the alphabet and is a non-connector, that is, it doesn't connect to the following character. Because **alif** is a non-connector, it has only two forms: an initial/independent and a medial/final form.

	medial/final	initial/independent
alif	ـا	ا

The pronunciation of **alif** depends on its position in a word. At the beginning of a word, it indicates the presence of one of the three short vowels, **a**, **i**, **u**. When joined to a preceding consonant, it represents a long **ā** vowel (as in the word 'father')

اَب	اِب	اُب
ab	**ib**	**ub**

بال

bāl (*hair*, m)

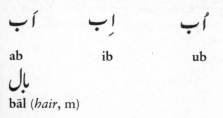

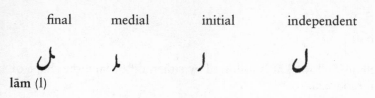

لال
lāl (*red*)

When **alif** follows **kāf** is followed by either **alif** or **lām**, the shape of **kāf** is modified.

کا
kā (*'s*)

کل
kal (*yesterday/tomorrow*)

Now see if you can read the following words:

بل	بال	کل	کال	اَب
bal	**bāl**	**kal**	**kāl**	**ab**
strength (m)	*hair* (m)	*yesterday/ tomorrow* (m)	*time/period* (m)	*now*

کلا	کالا	بلا	بالا	کب
kalā	**kālā**	**balā**	**bālā**	**kab**
art (f)	*black*	*calamity* (f)	*high/above*	*when*

The symbols in parentheses indicate whether a noun is masculine (m) or feminine (f). Every noun in Urdu is assigned one of these two grammatical genders.

Now that you have seen how easy it is to learn to read and write the **Nasta'līq** script, it is time to turn to Unit 1 of *Read and write Urdu script* and to start learning systematically the remaining characters in the Urdu alphabet. With just a little practice, it will not be long before you are well on your way to reading and writing Urdu fluently and ready to go on to learn the language proper, without the need for messy transliteration schemes.

Introduction

The Urdu script

The Urdu language is written in a modified form of the Persian script which is in turn a modified form of the Arabic script. This modification takes the form of the addition of characters to represent sounds that occur in Urdu but are not found in Arabic or Persian. In addition to Urdu, Persian and Arabic, the same script is used to write several other languages in India, Pakistan and Afghanistan, including Kashmiri, Punjabi and Pashto. There are two styles of this script: **Nasta'līq** and **Naskh**. The basic difference between these styles is minor. Whereas in **Naskh** words tend to run along the bottom line, in the more cursive **Nasta'līq** style they tend to slant diagonally from the top line to the bottom line.

السّلام علیکم	السّلام علیکم
Nasta'līq	**Naskh**

While the **Naskh** style of writing lends itself to type printing, texts written in the **Nasta'līq** style are still mostly prepared by a calligrapher and then printed using a technique called lithography. More recently **Naskh** and **Nasta'līq** fonts have been developed for use in computer software programs. The **Nasta'līq** style is conventionally employed in most Urdu texts, although the **Naskh** style, which is used to write both Arabic and Persian, is occasionally used in some scholarly publications and reference books. Because of the continued predominance of **Nasta'līq** to write Urdu, it is this style with which the student will have to become most familiar and which is, therefore, treated in this book.

The Urdu script runs from right to left except for numerals, which are written from left to right. The alphabet contains thirty-five characters, each of which possesses a name. For example, the first character in the alphabet is called **alif** and is used to represent several vowel sounds in Urdu.

ا
alif

The script is cursive, in that the characters are joined together to form words. There are no capital letters. Most characters are made up of a basic linear portion and one, two, or three dots or another symbol that resembles a 'flat' symbol in music. These are written either above or below the linear portion of the character. The basic shapes of some of the characters are the same and, for this reason, the alphabet is traditionally arranged in a series of characters that have a similar basic form but are differentiated by the number or position of accompanying dots, etc. For example, the second series of the alphabet comprises five characters, all of which have the same shape but a different number of dots or the symbol that resembles a flat sign in music.

ث 5	ٹ 4	ت 3	پ 2	ب 1
se	**ṭe**	**te**	**pe**	**be**

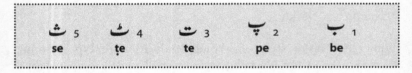

While all characters join to the preceding character in a word, not all join to the character that follows. Therefore, characters are conventionally considered to be of two types: those that join to characters on both sides and those that join only to the preceding character. Characters that join on both sides are called **connectors** while those that join only to the preceding character are called **non-connectors**. The shape of connecting characters also varies more or less depending on whether they occur at the beginning, in the middle or at the end of a word. There is also an independent form of characters, which occurs at the end of a word following a non-connector. It is the independent form that appears in the alphabet. Characters that do not connect to the following character have essentially only two forms: an initial and a final form. The initial form is the same as the independent form because it does not join to the following character and the final form is the same as the medial form for the same reason.

Another important feature of this script is that there are no characters to represent the three short vowels in Urdu. This makes learning how to pronounce new words difficult. There are, however, three symbols that may be employed to indicate which of these short vowels is present. There is also a symbol that is used to indicate when no vowel is pronounced with a character. These four symbols are rarely provided by writers because Urdu readers simply know the pronunciation of many of the words they read. However, they are always included in the Holy Quran to guarantee accurate pronunciation as well as in children's primers and dictionaries. They have also been used throughout this book with new words wherever they appear. Other features of the Urdu script include both the existence of several characters that represent more or less the same sound for Urdu speakers and also characters that may represent more than one sound. For example, there are four characters that represent the sound **z** and two characters that may each represent three vowels and a semi-vowel. There also exist some characters, the pronunciation of which is almost silent in particular words.

Some of these unique features can be explained by the fact that the Arabic script came to be used to write a language that evolved in the subcontinent, a long distance from where the script originated in the Middle East. How this came about is in turn related to the history of Muslim influence in the subcontinent and the evolution of languages and literary traditions in the places where Muslims settled in India and ruled from around the 14th until the 18th century. For Indian Muslims, Arabic maintained its importance as the sacred language of the Holy Quran and Persian continued to be an important spoken language as well as the language of administration and literary expression for much of this time. Over time a new language began to evolve, however, which was based on the dialect spoken in the north around Delhi but greatly influenced by Persian and Arabic. This influence came mostly in the form of the adoption of Arabic and Persian words and, eventually, the use of a modified form of the Persian script for writing purposes. In particular, new characters were added to this script to represent sounds that did not exist in Persian and Arabic and some of the distinctly Arabic and Persian sounds represented by particular characters were gradually diluted over time by speakers of this new language. The spellings of Persian and Arabic words have, however, remained faithful to the original. Hence the existence of different letters in the script representing the same sounds. The language that evolved, based on the dialect spoken in and around Delhi and enhanced by literary traditions in places such as Hyderabad in the south, came to be known as **rekhtā** ('mixed speech') as well as **zabān-e-urdū-e-mu'allā** ('the speech of the royal camps'). It was this second term which was finally abbreviated to provide Urdu with its modern name.

Many of the features of the Arabic script, and the anomalies that exist on account of its being applied to write Urdu, make learning to read and write this script a challenging task. It is for this reason that this book has been prepared. It is devoted entirely to the Urdu script rather than to the actual language, to give the student the opportunity to focus on learning to recognize the characters, both independently and when they occur in words. It is aimed at those with no previous knowledge of Urdu as well as those who can speak Urdu but cannot read or write it. The thirty-five characters are introduced gradually throughout the book and in an order that highlights those aspects of the script that are most likely to cause problems. Characters have not been introduced in the order in which they appear in the alphabet or in the conventional order in which they are taught. Rather, characters that are similar in shape have been deliberately spread over the chapters to focus attention on their differences rather than on their similarities. Because the book is also designed to help the student learn to write the characters, their formation is clearly detailed. There are also instructions on how to form whole words. These are designed to give the student a sense of the correct proportion of characters in relation to each other in a word and a feel for the flow of words when writing in Urdu. As far as possible, the words included in this book are generally commonly used and it is hoped that this may assist the student in developing a basic vocabulary. This will be of use when he or she goes on to learn the language proper. Finally, a modified form of the Roman script has been used to indicate the pronunciation of particular sounds in Urdu. This means that some of the letters included are marked by macrons (¯) or tildes (˜), e.g. ā, ẽ, ā̃, or dots underneath. A macron indicates a long vowel, a tilde indicates that a vowel is pronounced through the nose and a dot under a consonant indicates that it is pronounced by placing the tip of the tongue on the roof of the mouth (e.g. ḍ, ṭ, ṛ). At the end of this introduction, all of the characters in the Urdu alphabet are provided, both in the order in which they are introduced in this book as well as their dictionary order. This will be a useful guide for quick reference while working through the chapters. Also included is a chart showing all of the other symbols that are explained and the chapter in which they first appear. There is also a reference section in which other useful materials for the study of Urdu are listed.

Several people have contributed to the production of this book and I would like to thank them for their time and efforts. I am particularly indebted to Jeananne Webber who read through the entire manuscript with great attention to detail; Rashid Sultan Sahib provided valuable comments and criticisms concerning the structure and content of the book; Belinda Greenwood-Smith, Ralph Saubern, John Robinson, Novi Djenar, Lidia Tanaka, Sunil Sharma and Sudha Joshi all commented on various parts of the text, and the Department of Asian Studies, La Trobe University, Bundoora, provided me with the facilities to complete this manuscript. I am also thankful to the students who have tested out these materials in various forms, in particular Francesca Gaiba at the University of Illinois, Chicago. I am solely responsible for all errors and inaccuracies.

Characters of the Urdu alphabet

Order used in this book

Unit	Name of Character	Final form (un-joined)	Final form (joined)	Medial form	Initial form	Translit-eration
1	**be**	ب	ـب	ـبـ	بـ	**b**
	kāf	ک	ـک	ـکـ	کـ	**k**
	lām	ل	ـل	ـلـ	لـ	**l**
	mīm	م	ـم	ـمـ	مـ	**m**
2	**alif**	ا	ـا	ـا	ا	**a, i, u, ā**
3	**pe**	پ	ـپ	ـپـ	پـ	**p**
	jīm	ج	ـج	ـجـ	جـ	**j**
	gāf	گ	ـگ	ـگـ	گـ	**g**
	choṭī he	ہ	ـہ	ـہـ	ہـ	**h**
4	**ye**	ی	ـے ـی	ـیـ	یـ	**ī, e, ai, y**
5	**te**	ت	ـت	ـتـ	تـ	**t**
	ce	چ	ـچ	ـچـ	چـ	**c**
	sīn	س	ـس	ـسـ	سـ	**s**

	nūn	ن	ـن	ـنـ	نـ	n
6	vāo	و	ـو	ـو	و	ū, o, au, v
7	dāl	د	ـد	ـد	د	d
	re	ر	ـر	ـر	ر	r
	baṛī he	ح	ـح	ـحـ	حـ	h
	shīn	ش	ـش	ـشـ	شـ	sh
	svād	ص	ـص	ـصـ	صـ	s
8	zāl	ذ	ـذ	ـذ	ذ	z
	ze	ز	ـز	ـز	ز	z
	khe	خ	ـخ	ـخـ	خـ	kh
	zād	ض	ـض	ـضـ	ضـ	z
	fe	ف	ـف	ـفـ	فـ	f
9	ṭe	ٹ	ـٹ	ـٹـ	ٹـ	ṭ
	ḍāl	ڈ	ـڈ	ـڈ	ڈ	ḍ
	ṛe	ڑ	ـڑ	ـڑ	ڑ	ṛ
	ghain	غ	ـغ	ـغـ	غـ	gh

	qāf	ق	ـق	ـقـ	قـ	**q**
10	**se**	ث	ـث	ـثـ	ثـ	**s**
	zhe	ژ	ـژ	ـژ	ژ	**z**
	to’e	ط	ـط	ـطـ	طـ	**t**
	zo’e	ظ	ـظ	ـظـ	ظـ	**z**
	‘ain	ع	ـع	ـعـ	عـ	**‘**

Other symbols

Unit	Symbol	Name	Description
1, 4	ـَ	**zabar**	indicates a short **a** vowel as well as the vowels **ai** and **au** when used with the characters ا **alif**, ی **ye** and و **vāo**.
1, 4	ـِ	**zer**	denotes a short **i** vowel and is also used with the character ی **ye** to denote a long **ī** vowel. It is positioned under the character.
1, 5	ـُ	**pesh**	denotes a short **u** vowel and is also used with the character و **vāo** to indicate a long ū vowel. It is positioned above the character.
1	ـْ	**jazm**	indicates that a short vowel is not pronounced with a character. It is positioned above the character.

1	ّ	**tashdīd**	indicates that a character is repeated without an intervening vowel sound. It is positioned above the character.
2	~	**madd**	placed above ا **alif** when in an initial position to represent the long vowel **ā**.
2	کا		irregular initial and medial forms of the character ک **kāf** with ا **alif** and ل **lām**.
3	ھ	**do cashmī he**	denotes that a character is aspirated (i.e. produced with a breath of air).
4	گا		irregular initial and medial forms of the character گ **gāf** with ا **alif** and ل **lām**.
11	ء	**hamzā**	indicates that one syllable in a word ends with a vowel and the next begins with one.

Urdu alphabet in dictionary order

ا
alif

ب	پ	ت	ٹ	ث
be	**pe**	**te**	**ṭe**	**se**

ج	چ	ح	خ
jīm	**ce**	**baṛī he**	**khe**

(Continued)

د	ڈ	ذ	ر	ڑ	ز	ژ	
dāl	ḍāl	zāl	re	ṛe	ze	zhe	
س	ش	ص	ض	ط	ظ	ع	غ
sīn	shīn	svād	zād	to'e	zo'e	'ain	ghain
ف	ق	ک	گ	ل	م	ن	
fe	qāf	kāf	gāf	lām	mīm	nūn	
و	ہ	ی					
vāo	choṭī he	ye					

Vowel sounds in Urdu

There are ten vowel sounds in Urdu, three short and seven long vowels. The following chart shows the characters that are used to represent these sounds in particular positions in a word.

Vowel sound	Initial	Medial	Final
a (in **a**go)	ا alif	َ zabar	
ā (in f**a**ther)	آ alif + madd	ا alif	ا alif
i (in b**i**t)	اِ alif + zer	ِ zer	
u (in p**u**t)	اُ alif + pesh	ُ pesh	
ī (in b**ee**t)	اِیـ alif + ye + zer	ـِیـ ye + zer	ی ye

e (bet)	ایـ **alif + ye**	ـیـ **ye**	ے **ye**
ai (in h**a**y)	اَیـ **alif + ye+ zabar**	ـَیـ **ye + zabar**	ے **ye**
ū (in f**oo**d)	اُو **alif + vāo + pesh**	ـُو **vāo + pesh**	ـُو **vāo + pesh**
o (in g**o**)	او **alif + vāo**	ـو **vāo**	ـو **vāo**
au (in l**o**rd)	اَو **alif + vāo + zabar**	ـَو **vāo + zabar**	ـَو **vāo + zabar**

Useful reference materials

Barker, M. *et al.*, *A Course in Urdu* (New York: Spoken Languages Service, 1990)

Barz, R. and Yadav, Y., *An Introduction to Hindi and Urdu* (Delhi: Munshiram Manoharlal, 1993)

Delacy, R. and Joshi, S., *Elementary Hindi* (N.Clarendon, VT: Tuttle Publishing, 2009)

Ferozsons Urdu English Dictionary: a comprehensive dictionary of current vocabulary (Lahore: Ferozsons Ltd, 1987)

Matthews, D. and Dalvi, K., *Complete Urdu* (London: Hodder & Stoughton, 2010)

McGregor, R. S., *Outline of Hindi Grammar* (Oxford: Clarendon Press, 1987, second edn)

McGregor, R. S., *Urdu Study Materials* (Delhi: OUP, 1992)

McGregor, R. S. (ed.), *Oxford Hindi-English Dictionary* (Delhi: OUP, 1993)

Naim, C. M., Ahmad, Q.S., Nadvi, S.S., and Haq, M.A., *Introductory Urdu* (Chicago: Committee on South Asian Languages, University of Chicago, 1975)

Platts, J., *A Dictionary of Urdu, Classical Hindi and English* (London: OUP, 1960)

Russell, R., *A New Course in Urdu and Spoken Hindi* (London: School of Oriental and African Studies, London University, 1986)
Shackle, C. and Snell, R., *Hindi and Urdu since 1800: A Common Reader* (London: School of Oriental and African Studies, London University, 1990)
Zakir, M., *Lessons in Urdu Script* (Delhi: Idara-e-Amini, 1973)

Credits

Front cover: Oxford Illustrators Ltd

Back cover: © Jakub Semeniuk/iStockphoto.com, © Royalty-Free/Corbis, © agencyby/iStockphoto.com, © Andy Cook/iStockphoto.com, © Christopher Ewing/iStockphoto.com, © zebicho – Fotolia.com, © Geoffrey Holman/iStockphoto.com, © Photodisc/Getty Images, © James C. Pruitt/iStockphoto.com, © Mohamed Saber – Fotolia.com

Unit 1

In the introduction we saw that the Urdu alphabet contains thirty-five characters, each of which has a name. When these characters are joined together to create words, the form of many changes, depending on whether they appear at the beginning, in the middle or at the end of a word. The majority of characters join to both the preceding and the following character and, as a result, are known as **connecting characters**. Those that only join to the preceding character (but not to the following character) are called **non-connectors**. The four characters introduced in this unit are all connecting characters.

ب	ک	ل	م
be	**kāf**	**lām**	**mīm**

Pronunciation

These four characters represent consonant sounds.

Character	Name	Transliteration	Pronunciation
ب	**be**	**b**	**b** in **bin**
ک	**kāf**	**k**	**k** in **skip**
ل	**lām**	**l**	**l** in **long**
م	**mīm**	**m**	**m** in **man**

Positional forms

The shapes of each of these characters vary in four ways depending on their position in a word. Remember that the following table should be read from right to left.

Name	Final form (unjoined)	Final form (joined)	Medial form	Initial form	Transliteration
be	ب	ـب	ـبـ	بـ	**b**
kāf	ک	ـک	ـکـ	کـ	**k**
lām	ل	ـل	ـلـ	لـ	**l**
mīm	م	ـم	ـمـ	مـ	**m**

Writing practice

Each of the characters in the Urdu alphabet is formed in a precise manner and it is important to copy this exactly. Practise drawing the various forms of these four characters, following closely the guidelines given.

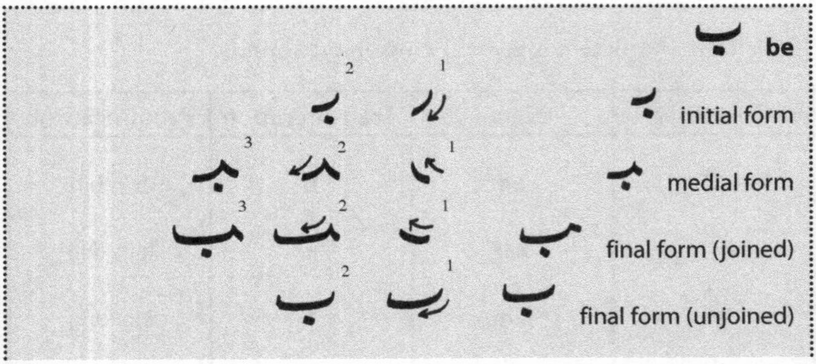

ک kāf

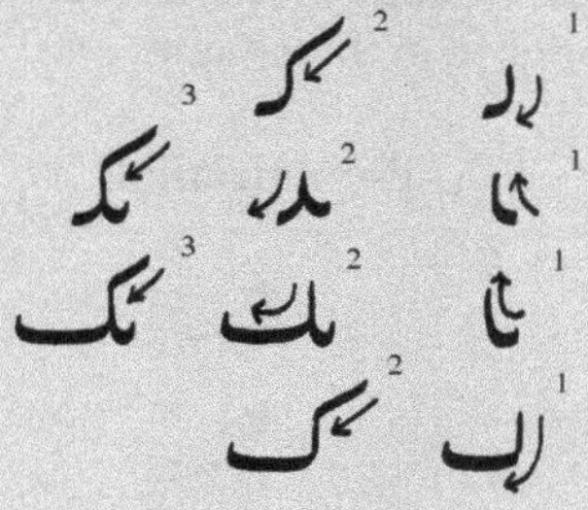

کـ initial form

ـکـ medial form

ـک final form (joined)

ک final form (unjoined)

ل lām

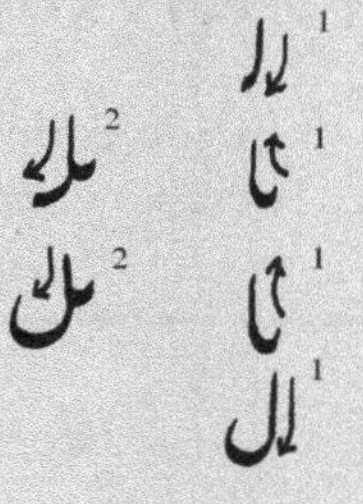

لـ initial form

ـلـ medial form

ـل final form (joined)

ل final form (unjoined)

م mīm

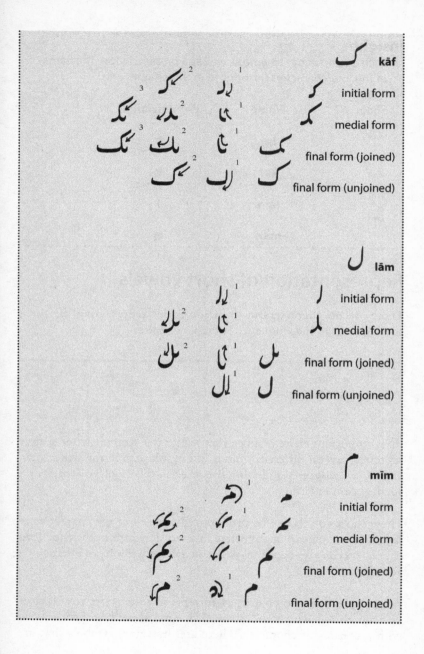

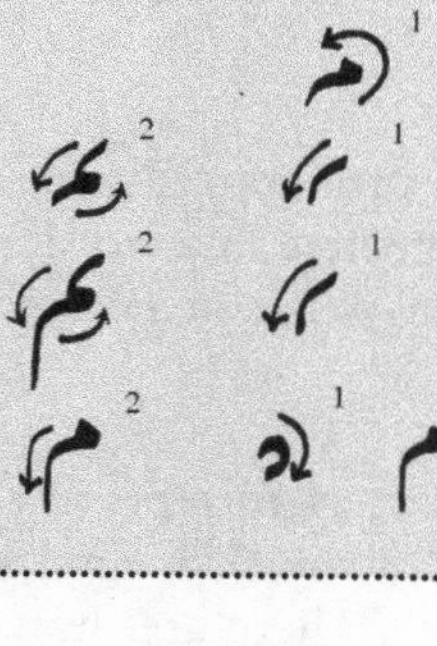

مـ initial form

ـمـ medial form

ـم final form (joined)

م final form (unjoined)

Insight

Each character has a name as well as a pronunciation. The names of the four characters introduced in this chapter are:

Shape	Name	Pronunciation
ب	**be**	**b**
ک	**kāf**	**k**
ل	**lām**	**l**
م	**mīm**	**m**

Representation of short vowels

There are no characters in the Urdu script representing the three short vowels in the language. These vowels are:

a in **a**go[1]
i in h**i**t
u in p**u**t

[1]It is important to remember that while the Roman letter a may represent several different sounds in English (e.g. in the words *ago*, *ate*, *arson*, *authority* and *ban*), it is used in this book to represent a single sound in Urdu.

These short vowels can be pronounced with all of the characters in the alphabet appearing anywhere in a word, except at the end. Two characters can also occur anywhere in a word without an intervening vowel sound.

Because there are no characters to represent the short vowels, it is difficult to tell which short vowel, if any, should be pronounced with a consonant character. There are, however, symbols that are employed, chiefly in dictionaries and children's primers, to clarify the pronunciation of words. These symbols represent the three short vowels and the omission of a vowel. These four symbols, written above and below characters, also possess names. They are:

َ	**zabar** (written above the character) = **a**
ِ	**zer** (written below the character) = **i**
ُ	**pesh** (written above the character) = **u**
ْ	**jazm** (written above the character) = no vowel[2]

[2]In some texts **jazm** appears as ° or ^.

These symbols, however, are not used in most Urdu texts except where the pronunciation of a word needs clarification. In this book only the symbols ِ **zer**, ُ **pesh**, indicating the short **i** and **u**, and ْ **jazm** are provided. ْ **jazm** is, however, never written above the final character in a word because, as a rule, a short vowel cannot be pronounced in this position. Where ِ **zer** or ُ **pesh** are not provided in a word, it is to be assumed that the character is pronounced with a short **a** vowel. For example, the pronunciation of three words made up of the initial form of the character ب **be** and the final form of the character ک **kāf** is clarified in the following manner:

بک	بِک	بُک
bak	**bik**	**buk**
nonsense (f)	*stem of the verb 'to be sold'*	*book* (f)

Insight

There are three short vowels in Urdu: **a** (as in '**a**go'), **i** (as in 'h**i**t'), **u** (as in 'p**u**t'). There are no characters to represent these vowels. They cannot occur at the end of a word.

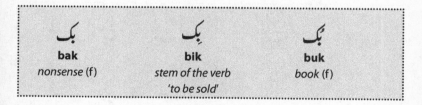

Reading and writing practice

1. Read the following words in Urdu and write them in Roman script. Remember that the short vowels i and u are marked by ِ **zer** and ُ **pesh**, that the absence of a vowel symbol indicates the presence of a short a vowel and that a short vowel is not pronounced at the end of a word.

Meaning	Roman	Urdu
strength (m)		بل (a
lip (m)		لب (b
mill (m)		مِل (c
less		کم (d
when		کب (e
book (f)		بُک (f

2. Practise forming these words according to the guidelines given.

strength (m)	 (a
lip (m)	 (b
mill (m)	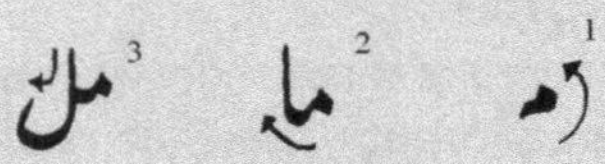 (c

less (d

when (e

book (f) (f

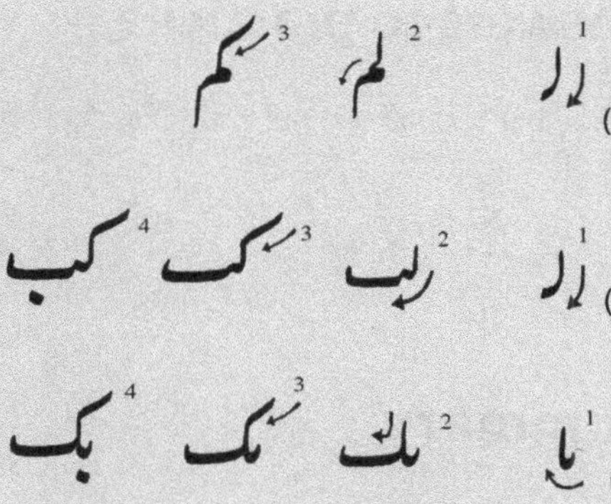

3. Connect the appropriate forms of the following characters to form the words. Remember to write in the short vowel symbols ِ **zer** and ُ **pesh** and the symbol ْ **jazm**, used to denote the omission of a vowel, where necessary.

Word	Characters	Roman	Meaning
	م + ل + ک =	**mulk**	*country* (m) (a
	ک + م + ل =	**kamal**	*lotus* (m) (b
	ک + م + ب + ل =	**kambal**	*blanket* (m) (c
	ب + ل + ب + ل =	**bulbul**	*nightingale* (m) (d

Insight

When writing words, it is best to write the linear portion first and then go back and fill in the dots and any diacritical marks.

ٮلٮل   بُلبُل   بُلْبُل

bulbul

Answers to practices

1. a) bal b) lab c) mil d) kam e) kab f) buk

3. a) مُلک b) کمل c) کُمبل d) بُلبُل

Summary

- The forms of most characters vary depending on whether they occur at the beginning, in the middle, at the end of a word or at the end after a non-connector.
- Each character has a name as well as a basic pronunciation.
- There are no characters to represent the three short vowels (**a**, **i**, **u**) in Urdu.
- There are four symbols occasionally employed to indicate the presence of a short vowel or the omission of a vowel (ـَ **zabar**, ـِ **zer**, ـُ **pesh** and ـْ **jazm**).
- Only the symbols ـِ **zer** and ـُ **pesh** are used in this book to represent short vowels.

Unit 2

In this unit the first non-connecting character is introduced. It is also the first character in the Urdu alphabet and represents four vowel sounds.

ا
alif

Positional forms

Non-connecting characters such as ا alif have only two forms, both of which are easy to recognize and draw.

Name	Final (joined) and medial form	Initial and final form (unjoined)	Transliteration
ا **alif**	ـا	ا	**ā, a, i, u**

Pronunciation

The pronunciation of ا alif depends on its position in a word.

Initial ا alif

In the absence of characters to represent the three short vowels in Urdu, ا alif is employed at the beginning of a word to indicate that it begins with one of these vowels. Occasionally the vowel symbols introduced in Unit 1 (َ **zabar**, ِ **zer** and ُ **pesh**) are used to clarify which of these vowels is present. In this book only the symbols for the short vowel **i**(ِ **zer**) and **u** (ُ **pesh**) are written in. An initial short **a** vowel is thus indicated by ا **alif** without a vowel symbol. For example:

اب	اِب	اُب
ab	**ib**	**ub**

Initial ا alif with the symbol ~ madd

ا **alif** also represents a long **ā** vowel at the beginning of a word. When it does, the symbol ~ **madd** is written (from right to left) above it.

Character	Name	Transliteration	Pronunciation
آ	**alif** and **madd**	**ā**[1]	**a** in f**a**ther

[1]The line above this letter in the Roman is used to distinguish this vowel sound from the short **a** (in ago) vowel introduced in Unit 1.

Medial ا alif

In the middle of a word ا **alif** represents a long **ā** vowel.

Character	Name	Transliteration	Pronunciation
ا	**alif**	**ā**	**a** in f**a**ther

For example:

اب	اِب	اُب	آب	با
ab	**ib**	**ub**	**āb**	**bā**

Insight

The character ا **alif** indicates the presence of a vowel. At the beginning of a word it can represent one of the three short vowels: **a**, **i**, or **u**. In the middle of a word, it represents a long **ā** vowel (as in 'f**a**ther').

Modified form of ک kāf

The initial and medial forms of ک **kāf** are written in a modified form when they are followed by either ا **alif** or ل **lām**. For example:

کا	=	ا	+	ک	کل	=	ل	+	ک
kā *'s*		**alif**		**kāf**	**kal** *yesterday/ tomorrow* (m)		**lām**		**kāf**

ّ tashdīd

The symbol ّ **tashdīd**, which looks very much like the letter **w**, represents the doubling of a character without an intervening vowel sound. It is written above the character that is repeated. For example:

اِکّا

ikkā
a one-horse vehicle (m)

Insight

A long **ā** vowel at the beginning of a word is represented by ا **alif** with the symbol ~ **madd** above it, written from right to left.

آ	آب
alif + madd	**āb** (*water*, m)

In the middle of a word, ا **alif** represents a long **ā** vowel:

باب

bāb (*chapter*, m)

Reading and writing practice

1. Practise forming the following words according to the guidelines given.

Roman	Urdu	Meaning
kal		*yesterday/ tomorrow* (m) (a
kām	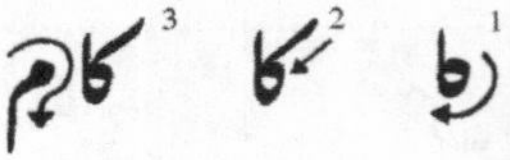	*work* (m) (b
mukkā		*fist, punch* (m) (c

2. Join the appropriate forms of the following characters.

Roman	Word	Characters
bā		= ا + ب (a
kā		= ا + ک (b
lā		= ا + ل (c
mā		= ا + م (d

3. Read the following words and write them in Roman script.

Meaning	Roman	Urdu
lotus (m)		کمل (a

hair (m)		بال (b
red		لال (c
tall, long		لَمبا (d
Muslim spiritual guide (m)		اِمام (e
black		کالا (f
collection of poetry (m)		کلام (g
bomb (m)		بم (h
mango (m)		آم (i
goods (m)		مال (j
maternal uncle (m)		ماما (k
a woman's name (f)		کُملا (l
complete		مُکمّل (m

4. Join the appropriate forms of the following characters to form the words given. Also write in the words any necessary short vowel symbols and ْ **jazm** (omission of vowel).

Word	Characters	Roman	Meaning
	آ + ب =	**āb**	*water* (m) (a
	ا + ب =	**ab**	*now* (b
	ل + ا + م =	**lām**	*name of character* (c
	ک + ا + م =	**kām**	*work* (m) (d
	ب + ل + ا =	**balā**	*calamity* (f) (e
	ک + ل + ا =	**kalā**	*art* (f) (f
	ب + ا + ل + ا =	**bālā**	*high, above* (g
	م + ا + ل + ا =	**mālā**	*necklace* (f) (h
	ل + ا + ل + ا =	**lālā**	*honorific title* (i
	ک + م + ا + ل =	**kamāl**	*miracle* (m) (j
	ک + ل + ا + ک =	**klāk**	*clock* (m) (k
	ا + ب + ا =	**abbā**	*father* (m) (l

5. Read the following phrases in Urdu and then write them in Roman script.

Meaning	Roman	Urdu
black blanket (m)		کالا کمُبل (a
red lotus (m)		لال کمل (b

complete work (m)		مُکمّل کام	(c
less work (m)		کم کام	(d
a long hair (m)		لُمبا بال	(e
yesterday/tomorrow's work (m)		کل کا کام	(f
uncle's miracle (m)		ماما کا کمال	(g
the Imam's work (m)		اِمام کا کام	(h
father's mango (m)		ابّا کا آم	(i

Insight

ک **kāf** has a modified form when *followed* by either ا **alif** or ل **lām**.

کب	کل	کا
kab (*when*)	**kal** (*yesterday/tomorrow*, m)	**kā** (*'s*)

Answers to practices

2. a) با b) کا c) لا d) ما

3. a) kamal b) bāl c) lāl d) lambā e) imām f) kālā g) kalām h) bam i) ām j) māl k) māmā l) kamlā m) mukammal

4. a) آب b) اب c) لام d) کام e) بلا f) کلا

g) بالا h) مالا i) لالا j) کمال k) کُلاک l) ابّا

5. a) **kālā kambal** b) **lāl kamal** c) **mukammal kām** d) **kam kām** e) **lambā bāl** f) **kal kā kām** g) **māmā kā kamāl** h) **imām kā kām** i) **abbā kā ām**

Summary

- ا **alif** is a non-connector (i.e. does not join to the following character).
- ا **alif** is used to indicate a short vowel (**a, i, u**) at the beginning of a word.
- ا **alif** with ~ **madd** at the beginning of a word represents the long vowel **ā**.
- ا **alif** in the middle of a word also represents the long vowel **ā**.
- The form of the character ک **kāf** is modified when followed by ا **alif** or ل **lām**.
- The doubling of a character without an intervening vowel is represented by the symbol ّ **tashdīd**, written above the character.

Unit 3

The four characters introduced in this unit are all connecting characters representing consonant sounds. In addition to these, the symbol that represents aspiration (i.e. a breath of air expelled with a character) is described. The four characters are:

پ	ج	گ	ہ
pe	**jīm**	**gāf**	**choṭī he**

Pronunciation

Character	Name	Transliteration	Pronunciation
پ	**pe**	**p**	**p** in s**p**in
ج	**jīm**	**j**	**j** in **j**ump
گ	**gāf**	**g**	**g** in **g**un (never as in **g**in)
ہ	**choṭī he**	**h**	**h** in **h**ut

In some words a short a vowel followed by ہ **choṭī he** at the end of a word are pronounced together as a long ā vowel. They are also occasionally pronounced as a short i or e vowel. Where such words are introduced in this book, first the Roman transliteration is given and then the pronunciation in parentheses. For example:

کلمہ

kalmah[1] (kalmā)

the expression of faith of a Muslim (m) (*'there is no God but Allah . . .'*)

[1]See below for the final form of ہ choṭī he.

Positional forms

Being connectors, all of these characters have four forms. پ pe and گ gāf have the same basic shape as the characters ب be and ک kāf, introduced in Unit 1. Because of this similarity both sets of characters are traditionally considered part of the same series in the Urdu alphabet.

Name	Final form (unjoined)	Final form (joined)	Medial form	Initial form	Transliteration
pe	پ	ـپ	ـپـ	پـ	**p**
jīm	ج	ـج	ـجـ	جـ	**j**
gāf	گ	ـگ	ـگـ	گـ	**g**
choṭī he	ہ	ـہ	ـہـ	ہـ	**h**

Writing practice

Practise drawing the various forms of the four characters introduced in this unit according to the guidelines given.

پ **pe**

For a description of how to draw the character پ **pe**, see the formation of ب **be** in Unit 1.

ج **jīm**

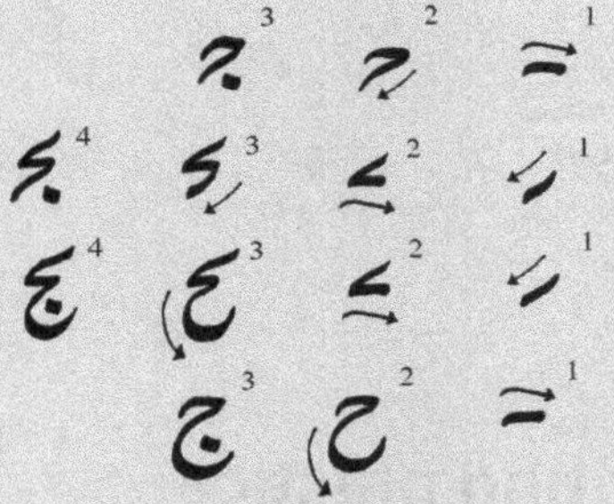

ﺟ initial form

ﺠ medial form

ﺞ final form (joined)

ج final form (unjoined)

گ **gāf**

For a description of how to draw the character گ **gāf**, see the formation of ک **kāf** in Unit 1. The second stroke at the top of the character is drawn the same way as the first, i.e. downwards.

ہ **choṭī he**

There are two initial forms of the character **choṭī he**: ہ **choṭī he** when joined to ا **alif** and when joined to any other character.

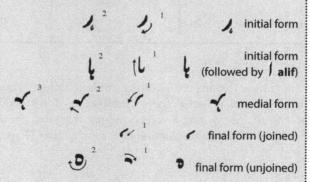

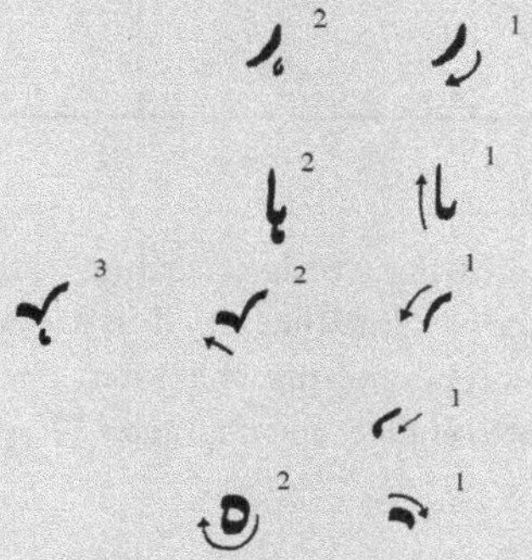

ﮨ initial form

ہا initial form (followed by ا **alif**)

ﮩ medial form

ﮧ final form (joined)

ہ final form (unjoined)

Modified form of گ gāf

As with ک kāf, the initial and medial forms of the character گ gāf also appear in a modified form when followed by either ا alif or ل lām. For example:

گا =	ا +	گ	گل =	ل +	گ
gā	**alif**	**gāf**	**gul**	**lām**	**gāf**
stem of the verb 'to sing'			*flower* (m)		

Reading and writing practice

1. Read the following words and then write them in Roman script.

Meaning	Roman	Urdu
you (polite)		آپ (a
today		آج (b
fire (f)		آگ (c
a sigh (f)		آہ (d

2. Practise forming the following words according to the guidelines and then write them in Roman script. Note that any dots are added to a portion of a word after writing a non-connecting character. For example, in the first word the three dots that complete the character پ pe are added after

drawing ا alif but before beginning the character ک kāf. If more than one character with dots occurs in a word, the dots are completed from right to left.

Roman	Urdu	Meaning
	1 ٮا 2 پا 3 پاک 4 پاک	*pure* (a
	1 ح 2 حا 3 جا 4 جام	*drinking vessel* (m) (b
	1 ٮا 2 کا 3 گا 4 گال	*cheek* (m) (c
	1 ٮا 2 ہا 3 ہال	*hall* (m) (d

3. Join the appropriate forms of the following characters to form the words given.

Word	Characters	Roman	Meaning
	= ک + پ + ل	**lapak**	*leap* (f) (a
	= ا + ج + ب	**bajā**	*chimed* (b
	= ا + گ + ل	**lagā**	*attached* (c
	= ا + ہ + ک	**kahā**	*said* (d

4. Write out the full (unjoined final) forms of the characters that make up the following words and then provide their Roman equivalents.

Roman	Characters	Word	Meaning
	+	= گپ	*gossip* (f) (a
	+	= جج	*judge* (m) (b
	+	= جگ	*world* (m) (c
	+ +	= جگہ	*place* (f) (d

5. Select the appropriate forms of the characters provided and then join them to make the following words.

Word	Characters	Roman	Meaning
	گ + م + ل + ا =	**gamlā**	*flower pot* (m) (a
	پ + ا + گ + ل =	**pāgal**	*crazy* (b
	ل + گ + ا + م =	**lagām**	*reins* (f) (c
	پ + ب + ل + ک =	**pablik**	*public* (d
	ب + ج + ا + ج =	**bajāj**	*brand name of a scooter* (e
	پ + ا + پ =	**pāp**	*sin* (m) (f
	ہ + ل + ک + ا =	**halkā**	*light* (g
	ہ + ل + ا + ک =	**halāk**	*killed* (h

	گ + ل + ا =	**galā**	*throat* (m) (i
	ک + ل + ا =	**kalā**	*art* (f) (j

Insight

Remember that the characters ب **be** and پ **pe** have the same basic linear form.

پل | بل | آب | آپ
pal (*moment*, m) | **bal** (*strength*, m) | **āb** (*water*, m) | **āp** (*you*)

ک **kāf** and گ **gāf** also have a very similar shape:

کل | گل | پک
kal (*yesterday/tomorrow*, m) | **gul** (*flower*, m) | **pak** (stem of the verb *to cook*)

لگ
lag (stem of the verb *to be attached*)

Aspiration

A particular form of the character ہ **choṭī he** is also employed to indicate that a consonant character is pronounced with a breath of air (i.e. aspiration). An example of an aspirated consonant in English is the initial **p** in the word **pit**. Place your open palm approximately ten centimetres from your mouth and pronounce both **pit** and **spit**. Can you feel the breath of air which is expelled with the first **p**? The form of ہ **choṭī he** that indicates aspiration is called **do cashmī he**.

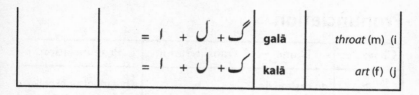

Pronunciation

Character	Name	Transliteration	Pronunciation
ھ	**do cashmī ḣe**	**h**	a breath of air expelled with a consonant

Writing practice

Practise forming the character **do cashmī he** according to the guidelines given.

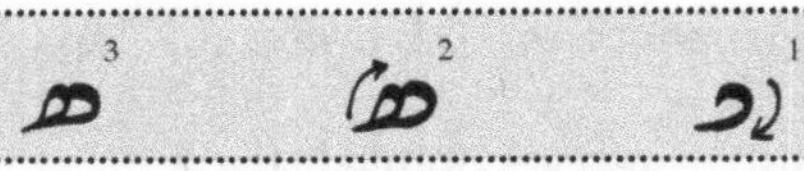

do cashmī he

Reading and writing practice

6. Write the following forms in Roman script.

(e	(d	(c	(b	(a
گا	کا	جا	پا	با
				Roman
(j	**(i**	**(h**	**(g**	**(f**
گھا	کھا	جھا	پھا	بھا
				Roman

7. Practise forming the following words according to the guidelines given.

Urdu	Roman	Meaning
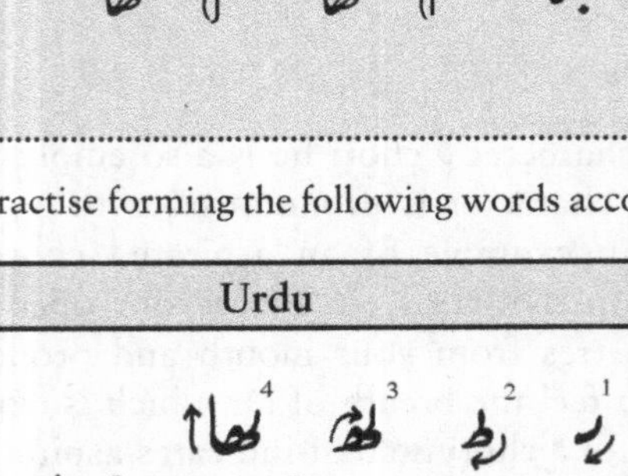	**bhāgā**	*fled* (a

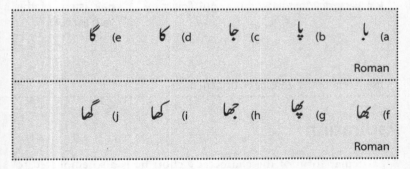

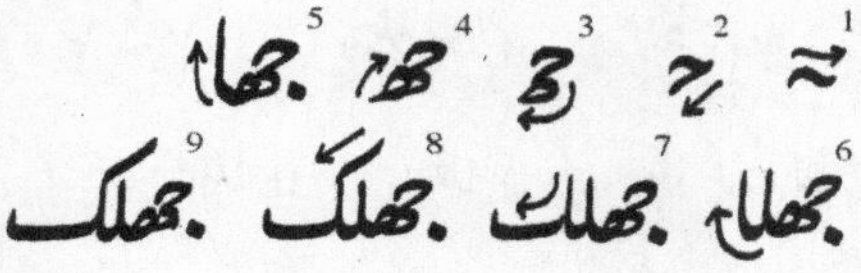	**jhalak**	*glimpse* (f) (b
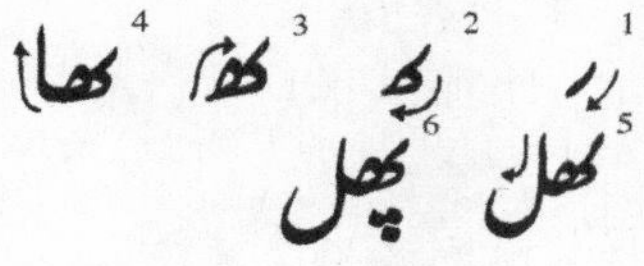	**phal**	*fruit* (m) (c
	**khāl**	*skin* (f) (d

Insight

When the character ہ **choṭī he** occurs at the end of a word, it is pronounced by some speakers as a long **ā** vowel.

کلمہ

kalmah (kalmā) (*the expression of faith of a Muslim*, m)

Answers to practices

1. a) āp b) āj c) āg d) āh

2. a) pāk b) jām c) gāl d) hāl

3. a) لپک b) بجا c) لگا d) کہا

4. a) گ پ gap b) ج ج jaj

   c) ج گ jag d) ج گ ہ jagah

5. a) گُملا b) پاگل c) لگام d) پبُلِک e) بجاج

f) پاپ g) ہُلکا h) ہلاک i) گلا j) کلا

6. a) bā b) pā c) jā d) kā e) gā f) bhā g) phā h) jhā i) khā j) ghā

Summary

- The characters پ **pe** and گ **gāf** have the same basic form as the characters ب **be** and ک **kāf**, introduced in Unit 1.

- Dots are added last or after a non-connecting character. If there is more than one character with dots in a word, they are added from right to left.

- There are two forms of the character ہ **choṭī he** in an initial position: ہ **choṭī he** with ا **alif** and ہ **choṭī he** with any other character.

- The character گ **gāf** has a modified form before ا **alif** or ل **lām**.

- A particular form of ہ **choṭī he** called **do cashmī he** ھ is used to indicate that a consonant character is aspirated (i.e. produced with a breath of air).

- Occasionally a short **a** vowel followed by ہ **choṭī he** in a word final position is pronounced as a long **ā** vowel.

Unit 4

Only one character is introduced in this unit. It is a connector and represents three long vowels and the semi-vowel y.

ی
ye

Positional forms

The basic shape of the initial and medial forms of the character ی ye is the same as that of ب be and پ pe, introduced in early units. This character also has two final forms which represent separate vowel sounds.

Name	Final form (unjoined)	Final form (joined)	Medial form	Initial form	Transliteration
ye	ی ے	ـی ـے	ـیـ	یـ	ī, e, ai, y

Writing practice

Practise drawing the various forms of this character according to the guidelines given.

			ی ye
	یر ۱	یـ ۲	یـ initial form
یر ۳	یر ۱	یر ۲	یـ medial form
ری ۲	یم ۱	یم ۲	ی final form (joined) (ī)
ے ۲	یر ۱	یر ۲	ے final form (joined) (e, ai)
ری ۲	یم ۱	یم ۲	ی final form (unjoined) (ī)
ے ۲	یر ۱	یر ۲	ے final form (unjoined) (e, ai)

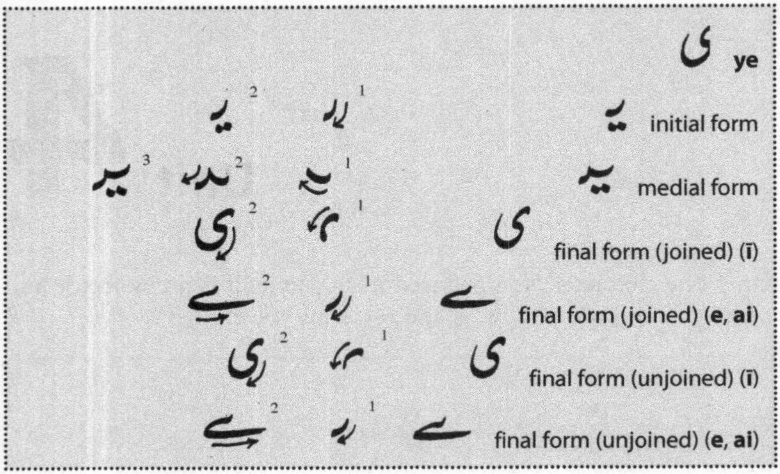

Pronunciation

The character ی ye represents three long vowels and the semi-vowel y.

Character	Name	Transliteration	Pronunciation
ی	ye	y	y in **yes**
		ī	ī in b**ee**t
		e	e in pl**a**y
		ai	**ai** in had

Word-initial ی ye

At the beginning of a word, ی ye represents the semi-vowel y. For example:

یا	یہ
yā	**yah**
	(ye)[1]
or	*this, he, she, it, they*

[1]The pronunciation of this word is exceptional. See the explanation of the pronunciation of ہ **choṭī he** at the end of a word in Unit 3.

Insight

There is a symbol that is used in dictionaries and primers to indicate the absence of a short vowel between two consonants in a word. It is called **jazm** (see Unit 1) and looks like a small comma: ْ .

ہلْکا

halkā (*light, not heavy*)

It is used in this book to clarify pronunciation.

Initial ī, e, ai vowels

When a long **ī**, e, or **ai** vowel occurs at the beginning of a word, it is represented by ی ye, preceded by the character ا alif. Occasionally the vowel symbol َ **zabar** is employed to indicate that it represents ai and ِ **zer** to indicate that it represents **ī**. The absence of these two vowel-markers thus indicates the presence of the vowel e.

اِیکھ	ایک	اَیسا
īkh	**ek**	**aisā**[2]
sugarcane (f)	*one*	*such/thus*

[2] سـ is the medial form of the character س **sīn**, which represents the consonant s. This is introduced in Unit 5.

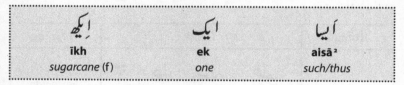

Medial ی ye

In the middle of a word ی ye may represent any one of the three long vowels and the semi-vowel **y**. Once again the vowel symbols َ **zabar** and ِ **zer** are occasionally used to indicate which of these sounds is present. When ی ye is followed by ا alif, it frequently represents the semi-vowel **y** or **iy** or even **īy**.

پیلا	کیلا	بَیل	بْیاہ	کْیا	کِیا	ایّام
pīlā	**kelā**	**bail**	**byāh**	**kyā**	**kiyā**	**ayyām**
yellow	*banana* (m)	*ox* (m)	*marriage* (m)	*what*	*did*	*days* (m)

Word-final ی ye

There are two forms of ی ye when it occurs at the end of a word: ی (i) and ے (e, ai). For example:

بے	ہے	جی
be	**hai**	**jī**
without (prefix)	*is/are*	*heart/mind* (m) (also a polite suffix)

Reading and writing practice

1. Follow the steps to form the following words and then write them out in Roman script.

Roman	Urdu	Meaning
	1 حـ 2 حلے 3 حلـ 4 حلیـ 5 حلیبی 6 جلیبی	*jalebi* (f) (a (*an Indian sweet*)

	1 ر 2 یک 3 یکا 4 یکا 5 یکاپر 6 یکایا 7 یکالک 8 یکانگ 9 یکایک	*suddenly* (b
	1 ر 2 لہ 3 لہج 4 لہجے 5 لہجے 6 لہجے	*accents* (m) (c

2. Read the following words and write them in Roman script.

Meaning	Roman	Urdu
even, also		بھی (a
drunk, drink		پی (b
take		لے (c
is/are		ہے (d
ghee (m) (*clarified butter*)		گھی (e
's		کے (f

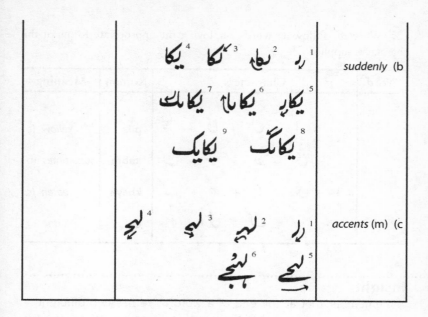

3. Write the following words employing the appropriate forms of the characters supplied.

Word	Characters	Roman	Meaning
	پ + ی + ل + ا =	**pīlā**	*yellow* (a
	ک + ب + ھ + ی =	**kabhī**	*sometimes* (b
	ک + ھ + ا + ی + ا =	**khāyā**	*eaten* (c
	ا + ی + ک =	**ek**	*one* (d

Insight

Remember that at the end of a word ی **ye** has two different forms. ے indicates that the vowel is either **e** or **ai**, whereas ی indicates that it should be a long **ī** vowel.

جی	لے	ہے
jī (*heart, mind,* m)	**le** (stem of the verb *to take*)	**hai** (*is/are*)

4. Read the following words, focusing on the differences that separate them, and then write them in Roman script.

بھلا	بلا	بالا	بال	بل	(a
good	*calamity* (f)	*above*	*hair* (m)	*strength* (m)	
					Roman
پھل	پلا	پالا	پال	پُل	(b
fruit (m)	*reared*	*nurtured*	*a sail* (m)	*bridge* (m)	
					Roman

جھل جھلا	جلا	جالا	جال	جل	(c
shining	*burnt*	*cobweb* (m)	*net* (m)	*water* (m)	
				Roman	

کھال	کلا	کالا	کال	کل	(d
skin (f)	*art* (f)	*black*	*period* (m)	*yesterday*	
				Roman	

گلا	گالا	گال	گُل	(e
throat (m)	*ball of cotton wool* (m)	*cheek* (m)	*flower* (m)	
			Roman	

گِیلا	پِیلا	جیل	کھیل	لیمپ	کیلا	(f
wet	*yellow*	*jail* (m/f)	*game* (m)	*lamp* (m)	*banana* (m)	
					Roman	

Punctuation

The most important punctuation marks used in Urdu sentences are shown below. Other punctuation marks are the same as the English.

؟	=	?
۔	=	.
،	=	,
؛	=	;

Reading and writing practice

5. It is now possible to read one or two sentences using some of the words you have learnt. Try to read the following sentences and write them

out in Roman script. It will help to know that the verb generally comes at the end of the sentence in Urdu. (The words in parentheses show the Urdu word order.)

Roman	Urdu	Meaning
	یہ کیا ہَے؟ *(is what this)*	*What is this?* (a
	یہ ایک پھل ہَے۔ *(is fruit one this)*	*This is a fruit.* (b
	کیا یہ آپ کی جلیبی ہَے؟ *(is jalebi your this)*	*Is this your jalebi?* (c
	یہ پیالا پیلا ہَے۔ *(is yellow cup this)*	*This cup is yellow.* (d
	کیا یہ آپ کی گلی ہَے؟ *(is alley your this)*	*Is this your alley?* (e
	آپ کا پیالا پیلا ہَے۔ *(is yellow cup your)*	*Your cup is yellow.* (f

Insight

When ی **ye** is followed by ا **alif**, it is likely to represent the semi-vowel **y**.

بیاہ

byāh (*wedding/marriage*, m)

Answers to practices

1. a) jalebī b) yakāyak c) lahje (lehje)

2. a) bhī b) pī c) le d) hai e) ghī f) ke

3. a) پیلا b) کبھی c) کھایا d) ایک

4. a) bal, bāl, bālā, balā, bhalā b) pul, pāl, pālā, palā, phal c) jal, jāl, jālā, jalā, jhalā jhal d) kal, kāl, kālā, kalā, khāl e) gul, gāl, gālā, galā f) kelā, laimp, khel, jel, pīlā, gīlā

5. a) yah (ye) kyā hai? b) yah (ye) ek phal hai c) kyā yah (ye) āp kī jalebī hai? d) yah (ye) pyālā pīlā hai e) kyā yah (ye) āp kī galī hai? f) āp kā pyālā pīlā hai

Summary

- The character ی ye represents three long vowels (i, e, ai) and the semi-vowel y.
- ی ye has two final forms ی (i) and ے (e, ai).
- At the beginning of a word the long vowels ī, e and ai are represented by ا alif and ی ye.
- The vowel symbol ِ zer is employed to mark that the character ی ye represents the vowel ī, while the vowel symbol َ zabar is employed to mark that it represents ai.
- The pronoun یہ yah (ye) (*he, she, it, this, they*) is pronounced irregularly.
- These Urdu punctuation marks are different from English:

؟	=	?	،	=	,
۔	=	.	؛	=	;

Unit 5

In this unit four connecting characters are introduced, one of which is also used to represent the nasalization of a vowel. These characters are:

ت	چ	س	ن
te	**ce**	**sīn**	**nūn**

Pronunciation

All four of these characters represent consonant sounds.

Character	Name	Transliteration	Pronunciation
ت	**te**	**t**	**t** in **t**on (the tip of the tongue touches the back of the top teeth)
چ	**ce**	**c**	**ch** in **ch**urch (never the **c** in **c**at)[1]
س	**sīn**	**s**	**s** in **s**un
ن	**nūn**	**n**	**n** in **n**ut

[1]Note that the sound **ch** is represented in the Roman by the letter c in this book. This is because there is an aspirated form of چ ce, which is represented in Roman script by **ch**.

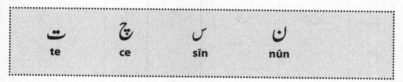

Positional forms

The basic form of the character ت te is the same as that of ب be and پ pe. The shape of چ ce is also identical to that of ج jīm, introduced in Unit 3. In both cases it is only the number of dots that differs.

Name	Final form (unjoined)	Final form (joined)	Medial form	Initial form	Transliteration
te	ت	ـت	ـتـ	تـ	**t**
ce	چ	ـچ	ـچـ	چـ	**c**
sīn	س	ـس	ـسـ	سـ	**s**
nūn	ن	ـن	ـنـ	نـ	**n**

Writing practice

Practise forming these new characters according to the guidelines given.

ت **te**

For a description of how to draw the character ت **te**, see the formation of ب **be** in Unit 1.

چ **ce**

For a description of how to draw the character چ **ce**, see the formation of ج **jīm** in Unit 3.

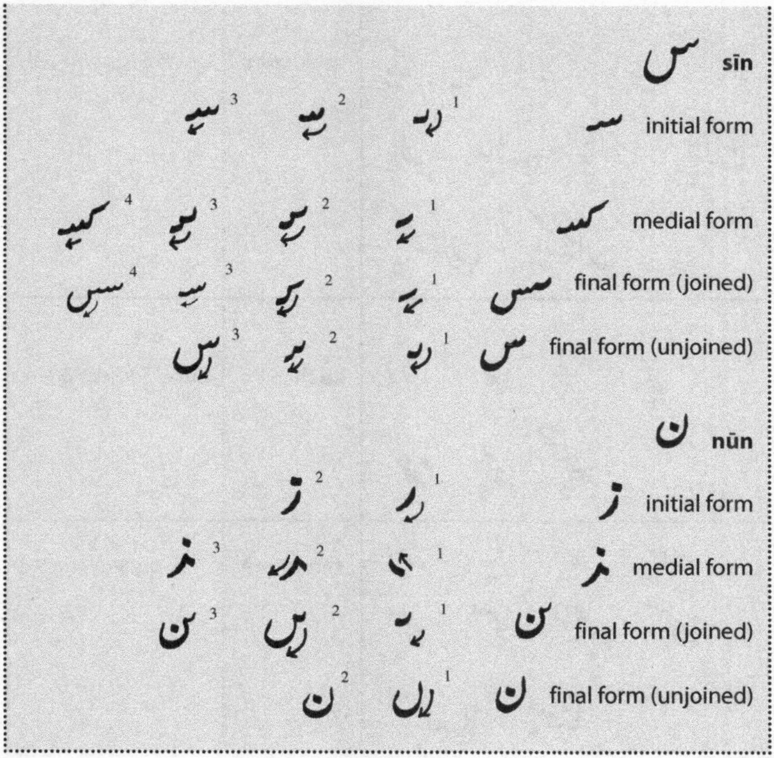

Reading and writing practice

1. Practise forming the following words according to the guidelines given.

Urdu	Roman	Meaning
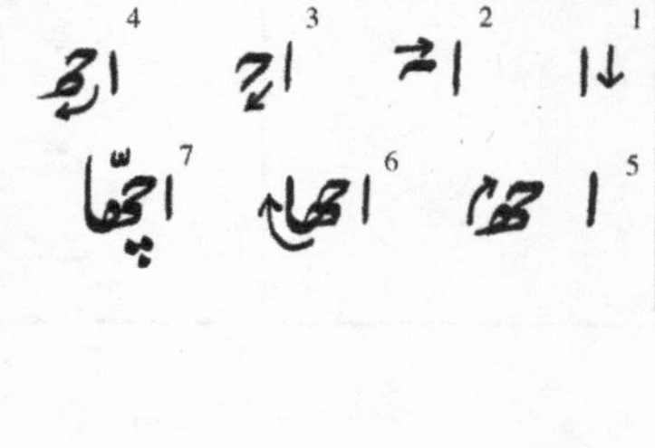	**acchā**	*good, okay* (a
		(*Continued*)

1 پا 2 پا 3 پال 4 پالیے 5 پالیے 6 پالسا 7 پالستا 8 پاکستا 9 پاکستان 10 پاکِستان	**pakistān**	*Pakistan* (m) (b
1 ل 2 ل 3 لچ 4 لچھ 5 لچھ 6 لچھ 7 کچھ	**kuch**	*some, something* (c
1 ر 2 سے 3 سم 4 سمے 5 سم 6 سمج 7 سمجھ 8 سمجھ 9 سمجھا 10 سمجھنا	**samajhnā**	*to understand* (d

2. Read the following words and write them in Roman script.

Meaning	Roman	Urdu
hand (m)		ہاتھ (a
conversation (f)		بات چِیت (b
smile (f)		مُسکان (c
from		سے (d
settlement (f)		بستی (e

3. Join the appropriate forms of the following characters to form the words given.

Words	Characters	Roman	Meaning
	ت + ی + ل =	**tel**	*oil* (m) (a
	ن + ا + م =	**nām**	*name* (m) (b
	چ + م + ک =	**camak**	*shine* (f) (c
	س + ا + ل =	**sāl**	*year* (m) (d

4. Complete the following words by placing the correct number of dots above or below the appropriate character.

a) ٮا **yā** *or*	b) ٮھا **thā** *was*	c) ٮاک **nāk** *nose* (f)	d) ٮھی **bhī** *also/even*
e) ٮاس **pās** *near*	f) حالاک **cālāk** *shrewd*	g) حھلک **jhalak** *glimpse* (f)	h) حھٮکلی **chipkalī** *lizard* (f)

5. Read the following words and write them in Roman script.

Meaning	Roman	Urdu
statement (m)		بیان (a
to tell		بتانا (b
to save		بچانا (c

(*Continued*)

to ring, strike			بجانا (d
heard			سُنا (e
assembly (f)			سبھا (f
Tuesday (m)			منگل (g
jungle (m)			جنگل (h
such			اَیسا (i
how			کَیسا (j

Insight

The character ت **te** belongs to the same series as the characters ب **be** and پ **pe** because of their identical linear portion.

ت	پ	ب
te	**pe**	**be**

There are two more characters in this series (introduced in later units).

Nasalization

The character ن **nūn** is also used to represent nasalization (the pronunciation of a vowel sound partly through the nose) in Urdu. In the middle of a word the medial form of ن **nūn** is employed (ﻨ) while at the end of a word the final form of ن **nūn** is written without the dot when it represents a nasalized vowel, i.e. ں. This particular final form of ن **nūn** is called **nūn ghunnā** (lit: 'talking through the nose'). In this book, the nasalization of a vowel is represented in Roman script by a tilde (˜) written above a vowel, e.g. **ã**. When trying to determine whether the character **nūn** in a medial position represents the nasalization of a vowel or the consonant **n**, it may help to remember that long vowels are often nasalized. For example:

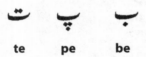

اِنسان	آنکھ	مان	ماں
insān	**ā̃kh**	**mān**	**mā̃**
human being (m)	*eye* (f)	*honour/respect* (m)	*mother* (f)

Occasionally the final form of ں **nūn** without the dot, representing nasalization, is found in the middle of a word. For example:

لِکھیں گے

or

لِکھینگے

likhẽge

he/they (m) *will write*

Insight

Remember that the characters ن **nūn** and ب **be** look remarkably similar in their initial and medial forms.

نل	بل	سُنا	تباہ
nal (*tap*, m)	**bal** (*strength*, m)	**sunā** (*heard*)	**tabāh** (*destroyed*)

It is only the position of the dot (above or below the line) that differentiates between them.

Nasalization is a very common feature in Urdu. Two commonly used words that are nasalized are the words for *yes* and *no*:

جی ہاں	جی نہیں
jī hā̃	**jī nahī̃**
yes	*no*

Insight

The word جی **jī** literally means *heart* or *mind* but is used here to soften the words and to add a degree of respect. It is also commonly used after people's names as a sign of respect.

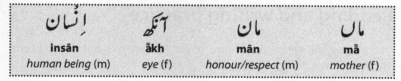

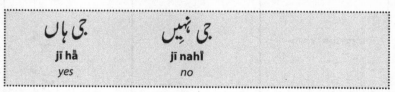

Reading and writing practice

6. Choose the appropriate forms of the following characters and form the words given.

Word	Characters	Roman	Meaning
	م + ی + ں =	**mẽ**	(a) *in*
	ی + ہ + ا + ں =	**yahā̃**	(b) *here*
	س + م + ج + ھ + ی + ں + گ + ی =	**samjhẽge**	(c) *will understand*

7. Read the following words and write them in Roman script.

Meaning	Roman	Urdu
where (?)		(a) کہاں
(*to*) *us*		(b) ہمیں
I (*first person pronoun*)		(c) مَیں
(*to*) *him/her/them*		(d) اُنھیں
books (f)		(e) کِتابیں

8. Read the following words quickly and then write them in Roman script.

(a

کِتنا	یکُساں	تھکُنا
how much (?)	*similar*	*to become tired*
		Roman
بتِّیس	کیتُلی	کیلا
thirty-two	*kettle* (f)	*banana* (m)
		Roman

(b

بنانا	کمُبل	کنُگال
to make	*blanket* (m)	*destitute*
		Roman
نتِیجہ	بتُلانا	نبی
conclusion (m)	*to tell*	*prophet* (m)
		Roman

(c

مجُلِس	جاپانی	چابی
party (f)	*Japanese*	*key* (f)
		Roman
سچ مچُ	سجانا	مچھُلی
really	*to decorate*	fish (f)
		Roman

Insight

Masculine nouns in Urdu that end in a long **ā** vowel change this to **e** to indicate the plural form. Masculine nouns that end in any other vowel or consonant do not change in the plural:

ایک کیلا	چار کیلے	ایک مکان	پانچ مکان
ek kelā	**cār kele**	**ek makān**	**pā̃c makān**
one banana (m)	*four bananas*	*one house* (m)	*five houses*

(There are other changes that take place to the ending of plural masculine nouns in other circumstances. These will be illustrated in later units.)

Answers to practices

2. a) hāth b) bāt cīt c) muskān d) se e) bastī

3. a) تیل b) نام c) چمک d) سال

4. a) یا b) تھا c) ناک d) بھی
 e) پاس f) چالاک g) جھلک h) چِھپکلی

5. a) bayān b) batānā c) bacānā d) bajānā e) sunā
 f) sabhā g) mangal h) jangal i) aisā j) kaisā

6. a) میں b) یہاں c) سمجھینگے

7. a) kahā̃ b) hamẽ c) maĩ d) unhẽ e) kitābẽ

8. a) thaknā, yaksā̃, kitnā, kelā, ketlī, battīs b) kangāl, kambal, banānā, nabī, batlānā, natījah (natījā) c) cābī, jāpānī, majlis, machlī, sajānā, sacmuc

Summary

- The character چ ce is represented by the letter **c** in Roman script. This is pronounced as **ch** in the word **church**.
- The basic form of ت te is the same as that of ب be and پ pe.
- The tip of the tongue touches the back of the top teeth when pronouncing ت te.
- The form of چ ce is the same as that of ج jīm.
- The initial and medial forms of ن **nūn** have the same basic shapes as those of the characters in the ب be series.
- The character ن **nūn** is also used to represent nasalization in Urdu. In the middle of a word the medial form of ن **nūn** is employed (ـنـ) while at the end of a word the final form of ن **nūn** is written without the dot when it represents a nasalized vowel (ں).

Unit 6

In this unit the character و vāo is introduced, a non-connector that represents three long vowels and a semi-vowel.

و
vāo

Positional forms

Because it does not connect to the following character in a word, و vāo, like ا alif, has only two forms, both of which are almost identical in appearance and easily recognizable.

Name	Medial and final form (joined)	Initial and final form (unjoined)	Transliteration
vāo	ـو	و	**ū, o, au, v**

Writing practice

Practise writing the two forms of the character و vāo following the guidelines.

و vāo

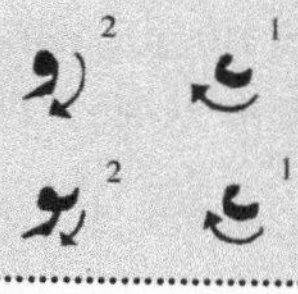

و initial and final form (unjoined)

ـو medial and final form (joined)

Pronunciation

The character و vāo may represent three vowel sounds and the semi-vowel v.

Character	Name	Transliteration	Pronunciation
و	**vāo**	**v**	somewhere between the English **v** and **w**. The upper teeth make slight contact with the back of the lower lip
		ū	**ū** in f**oo**d
		o	**o** in g**o** (without the **w** sound at the end)
		au	**au** in l**or**d

Word-initial و vāo

At the beginning of a word, و **vāo** represents the semi-vowel **v**. For example:

وجہ	وہاں
vajah	**vahā̃**
reason (f)	*there*

Initial ū, o, au vowels

The presence of one of the long vowels **ū**, **o**, **au** at the beginning of a word is marked by ا **alif** followed by و **vāo**. This combination of characters may, however, also represent a short vowel and the semi-vowel v. The vowels **ū** and **au** are occasionally distinguished using the short vowel-markers َ **zabar** (**au**) and ُ **pesh** (**ū**). This practice has been followed in this book. For example:

اُون	اولے	اَور	اوّل
ūn	**ole**	**aur**[1]	**avval**
wool (f)	*hailstones* (m)	*and*	*first, chief, best*

[1]The final character in this word is the independent form of the character ر re, which represents the consonant r.

Medial و vāo

In the middle of a word و vāo generally represents one of the three long vowels just described. Again, the short vowel signs may be employed to clarify which vowel is present. When و vāo is followed by either ا alif or ی ye, it often represents the semi-vowel v. For example:

تُو	تو	سَو	سوال	نوِیس
tū	**to**	**sau**	**savāl**	**navīs**
you	*then*	*one hundred*	*question* (m)	*writer/scribe* (m)

Insight

Feminine nouns that end in a consonant add a nasalized **ẽ** in the plural.

ایک کِتاب

ek kitāb (*one book*, f)

چھ کتابیں

cha (chai) kitābẽ (*six books*)

ایک آنکھ

ek ā̃kh (*one eye*, f)

چار آنکھیں

cār ā̃khẽ (*four eyes*)

Reading and writing practice

1. Following the guidelines given, write out these words. After you have done this, write their Roman equivalents.

Roman	Urdu	Meaning
	4 جوبا 3 جو 2 جو 1 ﺟ 6 جُوبلی 5 جوبلی	*jubilee* (f) (a
	5 جاسو 4 جاس 3 جا 2 جا 1 ﺟ 8 جاسُوس 7 جاسوس 6 جاسو	*spy* (m) (b
	4 بیوی 3 بیو 2 بیو 1 ﺑ	*wife* (f) (c
	5 بوجھ 4 بوج 3 بو 2 بو 1 بو 9 بوجھل 8 بوجھل 7 بوجھا 6 بوجھ	*heavy* (d

2. Read the following words and write them out in Roman script.

Meaning	Roman	Urdu
square (m)		(a چَوک
high		(b اُونچا

death (f)		مَوت (c
step-, half- (as in *step-sister*)		سَوتیلا (d

3. Join the appropriate forms of the following characters to make the words given.

Word	Characters	Roman	Meaning
	ج + و + ا + ن =	**javān**	*youth* (m) (a
	چ + ا + و + ل =	**cāval**	*rice* (m) (b
	س + م + و س + س + ا =	**samosā**	*samosa* (m) (c
	م + و + س + م =	**mausam**	*weather* (m) (d
	س + و + ک + ھ + ن + ا =	**sūkhnā**	*to dry* (e
	ک + ی + و + ں =	**kyõ**	*why* (?) (f

4. Write the full (unjoined final) forms of the characters that make up the following words.

Characters	Word	Roman	Meaning
+ + + + +	= مُسلمان	**musalmān**	*Muslim* (m) (a
+ + + +	= مَولوی	**maulvī**	*learned man* (m) (b

(*Continued*)

+ + + +	=	پینسِل	**pensil**	*pencil* (m)	(c
+ + + + + +	=	نَوجوان	**nau javān**	*young man* (m)	(d
+ + + + + +	=	ہُسپتال	**haspatāl**	*hospital* (m)	(e

Insight

Remember that a medial ن **nūn** could either be an **n** sound (nasal consonant), or a nasalized vowel. It is more likely to be a nasalized vowel when the vowel it follows is *long*.

آنکھ — **ā̃kh** (*eye*, f)

جنگل — **jangal** (*forest*, m)

5. Read the following phrases and write them in Roman script. Note that words that appear with vowel-markers (َ **zabar**, ِ **zer** and ُ **pesh**) or ْ **jasm** reappear without these symbols. This is designed to assist in recognizing words as they would appear in unedited texts.

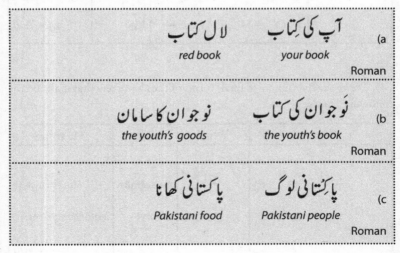

لال کتاب	آپ کی کِتاب	(a
red book	*your book*	
	Roman	
نوجوان کا سامان	نَوجوان کی کتاب	(b
the youth's goods	*the youth's book*	
	Roman	
پاکستانی کھانا	پاکِستانی لوگ	(c
Pakistani food	*Pakistani people*	
	Roman	

(d	کُچھ لوگ *some people*	کچھ کتابیں *some books*	کچھ پنجُابی لوگ *some Punjabi people*
Roman			
(e	پنجابی نوجوان *Punjabi youth*	پنجاب کا بینک *Punjab's bank*	بینک کا کام *bank('s) work*
Roman			
(f	ہسپتال کا کام *hospital('s) work*	ہسُپتال کا نام *the name of the hospital*	کتاب کا نام *the name of the book*
Roman			
(g	بینک کا نام *the name of the bank*	کِتُنا کام *how much work?*	کتنا پیَسہ *how much money?*
Roman			
(h	بہُت پیسہ *much money*	بہت لوگ *many people*	بہت پاکستانی لوگ *many Pakistani people*
Roman			
(i	مُسلُمان لوگ *Muslim people*	کچھ مسلمان *some Muslims*	مولُوی کا کام *the maulvi's work*
Roman			
(j	مولوی کا سامان *the maulvi's goods*	آپ کا بچُپن *your childhood*	بچپن کی بات *a childhood('s) matter*
Roman			

6. Read the following graffiti and translate it into English.

a) وہ بھی پاکستانی ہَے۔

b) آپ بھی پاکستانی ہَیں۔

c) ہم سب پاکستانی ہَیں۔

d) ہم سب کا مُلک ہے پاکستان۔

QUICK VOCAB

he/she/it/that (pronounced irregularly as **vo**)	وہ	*are*	ہَیں
also	بھی	*we*	ہم
is	ہَے	*all*	سب
you (polite)	آپ	*country* (m)	مُلک

Answers to practices

1. a) **jūblī** b) **jāsūs** c) **bīvī** d) **bojhal**

2. a) **cauk** b) **ū̃cā** c) **maut** d) **sautelā**

3. a) جوان b) چاول c) سموسا
   d) مَوسم e) سوُ کھنا f) کیوں

4. a) م س ل م ا ن muslamān
   b) م و ل و ی maulvī
   c) پ ی ن س ل pensil
   d) ن و ج و ا ن nau javān
   e) ہ س پ ت ا ل haspitāl

5. a) āp kī kitāb, lāl kitāb b) naujavān kī kitāb, naujavān kā sāmān c) pākistānī log, pākistānī khānā d) kuch log, kuch kitābẽ, kuch panjābī log e) panjābī naujavān, panjāb kā baink, baink kā kām f) haspatāl kā kām, haspatāl kā nām, kitāb kā nām g) baink kā nām, kitnā kām, kitnā paisah (paisā) h) bahut paisah (paisā), bahut log, bahut pākistānī log i) musalmān log, kuch musalmān, maulvī kā kām j) maulvī kā sāmān, āp kā bacpan, bacpan kī bāt

6. a) vah (vo) bhī pākistānī hai *he/she also is Pakistani* b) āp bhī pākistānī haĩ *You also are Pakistani* c) ham sab pākistānī haĩ *we are all Pakistani* d) ham sab kā mulk hai pākistān *Pakistan belongs to us all (we all's country is Pakistan)*

Summary

- و vāo represents three long vowel sounds and the semi-vowel v.
- At the beginning of a word, و vāo represents v.
- The three long vowels u, o, and au are represented at the beginning of a word by ا alif and و vāo.
- When و vāo is followed by either ا alif or ی ye in the middle of a word, it often represents the semi-vowel v.
- The pronunciation of the pronoun وہ vah (vo) (*he, she, it, that*) is irregular.

Unit 7

Five characters are introduced in this unit. This brings the total number of characters thus far to twenty. All five of these characters represent consonant sounds in Urdu. Three of these are connectors and two are non-connectors.

د	**dāl**	non-connector
ر	**re**	non-connector
ح	**baṛī he**	connector
ش	**shīn**	connector
ص	**svād**	connector

Pronunciation

For most Urdu speakers the pronunciation of the characters ح **baṛī he** and ص **svād** is almost exactly the same as that of ہ **choṭī he** and س **sīn**, introduced in earlier units. This is because the sounds that these characters represent in Arabic were gradually diluted in Urdu but the original spellings of words in which they occur have been maintained. For this reason, they are represented in Roman script in this book by the same letters (**h** and **s**). It is important to remember that the letter **h** is also used to represent the aspiration of a consonant.

Character	Name	Transliteration	Pronunciation
د	**dāl**	**d**	**d** in **d**one (the tip of the tongue touches the back of the top teeth)

(*Continued*)

ر	**re**	**r**	**r** in **r**un
ح	**baṛī he**	**h**	**h** in **h**ut
ش	**shīn**	**sh**	**sh** in **sh**un
ص	**svād**	**s**	**s** in **s**un

Insight

ح **baṛī he** belongs to the same series as ج **jīm** and چ **ce**, because of their similar linear shape. Take care not to confuse them.

ح	چ	ج
baṛī he	**ce**	**jīm**
حلال	چالاک	جھلک
halāl (*halal*)	**cālāk** (*shrewd, cunning*)	**jhalak** (*glimpse*, f)

Positional forms

It is often difficult for the beginner to distinguish between the non-connecting characters د dāl and ر re because of their similar shape. It will help to remember that د dāl joins to the preceding character at the middle whereas ر re joins at the top. These characters are also often confused with the character و vāo.

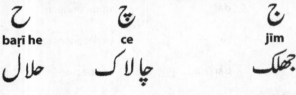

Name	Final form (unjoined)	Final form (joined)	Medial form	Initial form	Transliteration
dāl	د	ـد	ـد	د	**d**
re	ر	ـر	ـر	ر	**r**

baṛī he	ح	ـح	ـحـ	حـ	**h**
shīn	ش	ـش	ـشـ	شـ	**sh**
svād	ص	ـص	ـصـ	صـ	**s**

Writing practice

Practise forming these characters according to the guidelines given.

د dāl

د initial and final (unjoined) form

ـد medial and final (joined) form

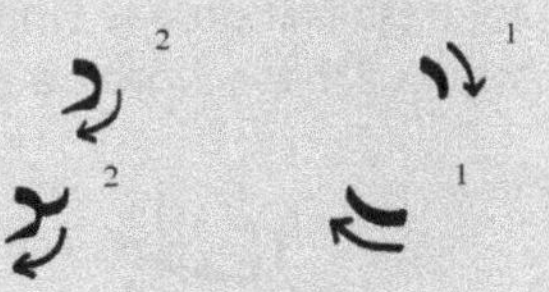

ر re

ر initial and final (unjoined) form

ـر medial and final (joined) form

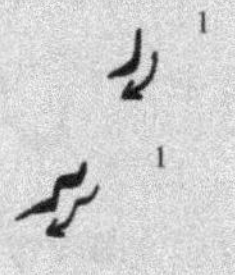

ح **baṛī he**

For a description of how to draw the forms of the character ح **baṛī he**, see the formation of ج **jīm** in Unit 3.

ش **shīn**

For a description of how to draw the forms of the character ش **shīn**, see the formation of س **sīn** in Unit 5.

ص **svād**

صـ initial form

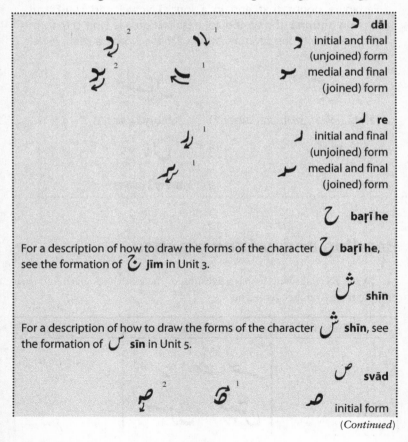

(*Continued*)

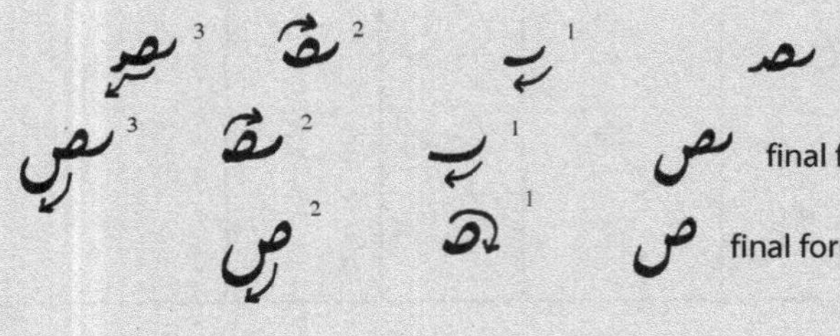

Insight

Feminine nouns that end in a long **ī** vowel add ا **alif** and ں **nūn ghunnā** (the symbol for nasalization, see Unit 5) to form their plurals. In the pronunciation of these words, a semi-vowel **y** is also expressed.

جلیبی	جلیبیاں
jalebī (*jalebi, an Indian sweet*, f)	**jalebiyā̃** (*jalebis*)
بیوی	بیویاں
bīvī (*wife*, f)	**bīviyā̃** (*wives*)

Reading and writing practice

1. Write the following words according to the guidelines given and then provide their Roman equivalents.

Roman	Urdu	Meaning
	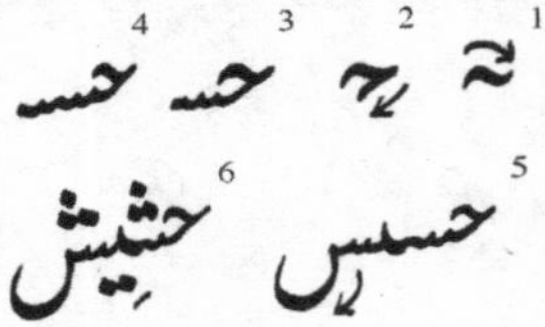	*hashish* (f) (a

	1 ھ 2 صد 3 صدر	*chairman* (m) (b
	1 یہ 2 ریہ 3 کریہ 4 شکریہ 5 شکر 6 شکریہ 7 شُکرِیہ	*thank you* (m) (c
	1 کا 2 نکا 3 نکا 4 نکا 5 نِکاح	*Muslim wedding ceremony* (m) (d
	1 ر 2 ویر 3 صویر 4 تصویر 5 تصویر 6 تصوِیر	*picture* (f) (e
	1 ھ 2 صح 3 صح 4 صحت 5 صحت	*health* (f) (f

2. Read the following words and write them in Roman script.

Meaning	Roman	Urdu
dhal (f)		دال (a
night (f)		رات (b

(*Continued*)

soap (m)		صابُن (c
ruler, governor (m)		حاکِم (d
splendour, lustre (f)		شان (e
washerman (m)		دھوبی (f
rail (f)		ریل (g
province (m)		صُوبہ (h
life, existence (f)		حیات (i
grandeur, dignity (f)		شَوکت (j

3. Join the appropriate forms of the characters supplied to form the following words.

Word	Characters	Roman	Meaning
	= د + ا + ب + آ	**ābād**	*populated* (a
	= م + ا + ر + آ	**ārām**	*rest/ respite* (m) (b
	= ی + م + د + آ	**ādmī**	*man* (m) (c
	= ر + گ + ا	**agar**	*if* (d
	= د + ح + ر + س	**sarhad**	*border* (f) (e
	= و + د + ر + ا	**urdū**	*Urdu* (f) (f
	= ش + ش + و + ک	**koshish**	*effort/ endeavour* (f) (g

4. Read the following words, focusing on the characters that are similar in shape, and then write them in Roman script.

(a	درد	دارُو	دو	رونا
	pain (m)	*medicine* (f)	*two*	*to cry*
Roman				
(b	اُردُو	دُوسرا	دونوں	دَور
	Urdu (f)	*second/other*	*both*	*tour* (m)
Roman				
(c	دُودھ	دھوبی	اِرادہ	بدُتر
	milk (m)	*washerman* (m)	*intention* (m)	*worse*
Roman				
(d	شب	سب	شاہ	سانپ
	night (f)	*all*	*ruler* (m)	*snake* (m)
Roman				
(e	دسُت	راسُتہ	دُشمن	رِشتہ
	hand (m)	*way/path* (m)	*enemy* (m)	*relation* (m)
Roman				
(f	حج	حد	حرام	
	pilgrimage (m)	*extreme/limit* (f)	*forbidden*	
	رُجحان	حرج		
	inclination (m)	*damage/loss* (m)		
Roman				

Insight

Remember that و **vāo** can be pronounced in a medial position either as a long **ū**, an **o**, or an **au** vowel sound. When followed by a long vowel, it is likely to be pronounced as the semi-vowel **v**.

لُو	لو	لَو	بِیوی
lū (*hot wind*, f)	**lo** (*to take*)	**lau** (*flame*, f)	**bīvī** (*wife*, f)

5. Read the following advertisement and translate it into English. A glossary of unfamiliar words can be found below.

a) پنجاب نیشنل بینک

b) لاہور

c) آپ کا بینک

d) آپ کے ساتھ

e) آج بھی کل بھی

f) ہمیشہ

g) بھروسے کا نِشان

QUICK VOCAB

Punjab	پنجاب	*today*	آج
national	نیشنل	*tomorrow*	کل
bank (m)	بینک	*forever*	ہمیشہ

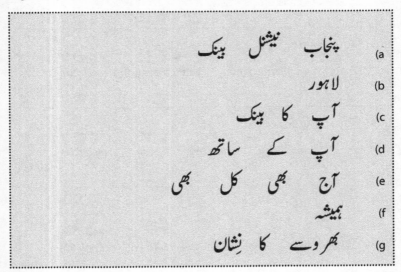

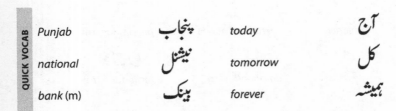

QUICK VOCAB

Lahore	لاہور	*reliance/trust* (m)	بھروسا
you	آپ	*sign* (m)	نِشان
with	کے ساتھ	*even/also*	بھی

Insight

Remember that the characters و **vāo**, د **dāl** and ر **re** look incredibly similar. For this reason they are often confused. All are non-connectors. Looking closely at where these characters connect to the preceding character may help you to recognize them.

مدد　　مرنا　　مَوت

madad (*assistance*, f)　**marnā** (*to die*)　**maut** (*death*, f)

د **dāl** attaches to the preceding character in the middle and is slightly angular, ر **re** attaches at the top and is curved, and و **vāo** looks more like a comma.

Answers to practices

1. a) **hashīsh** b) **sadar** c) **shukriyah (shukriyā)** d) **nikāh** e) **tasvīr** f) **sahat (sehat)**

2. a) **dāl** b) **rāt** c) **sābun** d) **hākim** e) **shān** f) **dhobī** g) **rel** h) **sūbah (sūbā)** i) **hayāt** j) **shaukat**

3. a) آباد b) آرام c) آدُمی d) اگر e) سرُحد f) اُردُو g) کوشِش

4. a) **dard, dārū, do, ronā** b) **urdū, dūsrā, donō, daur** c) **dūdh, dhobī, irādah (irādā), badtar** d) **shab, sab, shāh, sā̃p** e) **dast, rāstah (rāsta), dushman, rishtah (rishtā)** f) **haj, had, harām, rujhān, harj**

5. a) **panjāb neshanal baink** *Punjab National Bank* b) **lahaur** *Lahore* c) **āp kā baink** *your bank* d) **āp ke sāth** *with you* e) **āj bhī kal bhī** *today also tomorrow also* f) **hameshah** (**hameshā**) *forever* g) **bharose kā nishān** *the sign of reliance*

Summary

- The tip of the tongue touches the top of the back teeth in the pronunciation of د **dāl**.
- The characters ہ **choṭī he** and ح **baṛī he** represent the same sound for most speakers and are both represented in Roman script by the letter **h** in this book.
- س **sīn** and ص **svād** also represent the same sound and are both represented by **s** in Roman script in this book.
- د **dāl** and ر **re** are most easily distinguished by focusing on the point at which they join to the preceding character.
- ش **shīn** has the same basic shape as س **sīn**.
- The shape of ح **baṛī he** is the same as that of ج **jīm**. Therefore, they are grouped together in the alphabet.

Unit 8

The five characters introduced in this unit occur mainly in words that have come into Urdu from Persian, Arabic and English. Three are connectors and two are non-connectors. They are:

خ	**kh̲e**	connector
ذ	**zāl**	non-connector
ز	**ze**	non-connector
ض	**zād**	connector
ف	**fe**	connector

Pronunciation

Three of these five characters represent the same sound for most speakers of Urdu. As with the characters ح **baṛī he** and ص **svād** in Unit 7, the reason for this is that the Arabic phonetic values of the characters have been lost in Urdu but the original spellings of the words in which they occur have been retained.

Character	Name	Transliteration	Pronunciation
خ	**khe**	**kh**	similar to **ch** in the Scottish word lo**ch**
ذ	**zāl**		
ز	**ze**	**z**	**z** in **z**ebra
ض	**zād**		
ف	**fe**	**f**	**f** in **f**un

Positional forms

The basic shape of the character خ khe is the same as that of ج jīm and with the introduction of خ khe this series of characters is now complete (ج jīm, چ ce, ح baṛī he, and خ khe). The basic shapes of the characters ذ zāl and ز ze are the same as those of د dāl and ر re. For this reason they too belong to the same series. ض zād is identical in shape to ص svād. Finally the linear portion of the character ف fe is also similar to the basic shape of the **be** series of characters although it is not included with them in that series. The line under the Roman representation of the character خ khe is used to distinguish it from the aspirated form of the character ک kāf (کھ kh).

Name	Final form (unjoined)	Final form (joined)	Medial form	Initial form	Transliteration
khe	خ	ـخ	ـخـ	خـ	**kh**
zāl	ذ	ـذ	ـذ	ذ	**z**
ze	ز	ـز	ـز	ز	**z**

zād	ض	ـض	ـضـ	ضـ	z
fe	ف	ـف	ـفـ	فـ	f

Insight

With the introduction of the character خ **kh̲e**, the ج **jīm** series is now complete. All of these characters are traditionally grouped together in the alphabet because of their similar linear portion.

خ	ح	چ	ج
kh̲e	**baṛī he**	**ce**	**jīm**

ذ **zāl** has the same basic shape as د **dāl** and ز **ze** has the same basic shape as ر **re**. They are considered part of the same series.

ز	ر	ذ	د
ze	**re**	**zāl**	**dāl**

Writing practice

Practise writing the various forms of these characters.

خ **kh̲e**

For a description of how to draw the forms of the character خ **kh̲e**, see the formation of ج **jīm** in Unit 3.

ذ **zāl**

For a description of how to draw the forms of the character ذ **zāl**, see the formation of د **dāl** in Unit 7.

ز **ze**

For a description of how to draw the forms of the character ز **ze**, see the formation of ر **re** in Unit 7.

ض **zād**

For a description of how to draw the forms of the character ض **zād**, see the formation of ص **svād** in Unit 7.

ف **fe**

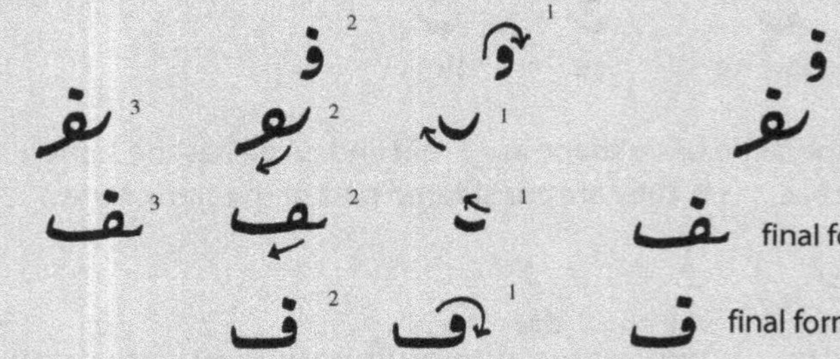

Reading and writing practice

1. Following the guidelines given, write these words in Urdu and then provide their Roman equivalents.

Roman	Urdu	Meaning
		*ostentation* (m) (a

	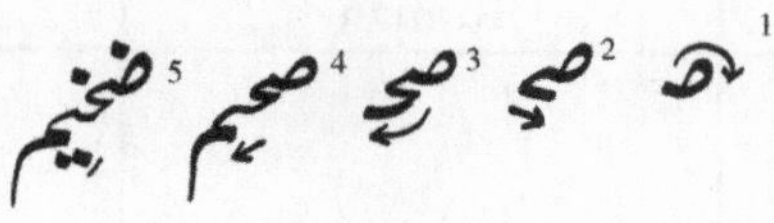	*fat* (b
	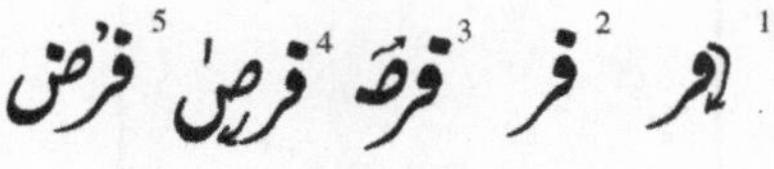	*duty* (m) (c
	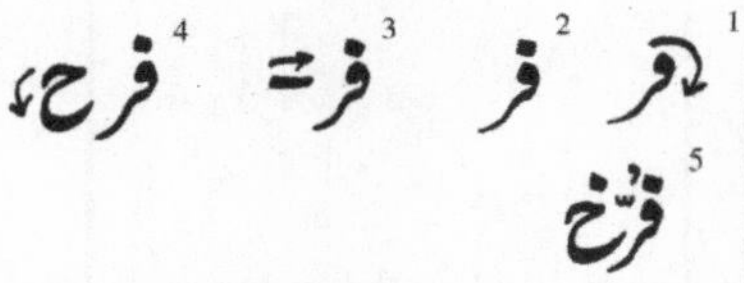	*beautiful* (d (also a name)

Insight

All nouns (masculine and feminine) possess a particular plural ending when they are used with words like 'in', 'on', 'with'. Called prepositions in English, such words *follow* the word they govern in Urdu and, hence, are called *post*positions. The ending for all nouns in the plural when used with postpositions is **õ**.

میں

mẽ means 'in'.

کمرا	کمروں میں
kamrā (*room*, m)	**kamrõ mẽ** (*in (the) rooms*)
کتاب	کتابوں میں
kitāb (*book*, f)	**kitābõ mẽ** (*in (the) books*)

When the masculine noun ends in a long **ā** vowel, this vowel is replaced by the **õ** suffix.

2. Read the following words and write them in Roman script.

Meaning	Roman	Urdu
special		خاص (a
fever (m)		بُخار (b
direction (m)		رُخ (c
a little		ذرا (d
religion (m)		مذہب (e
tasty		لذِیذ (f
a cold (m)		زُکام (g
elderly		بُزُرگ (h
thing (f)		چِیز (i
certainly		ضرُور (j
Sir!		حُضُور (k
a (water) tank (m)		حَوض (l
worry (f)		فِکر (m
journey (m)		سفر (n
clean		صاف (o

3. Join the appropriate forms of the characters supplied to write the following words.

Word	Characters	Roman	Meaning
	خ + ب + ر =	**<u>kh</u>abar**	news (f) (a
	ت + خ + ت =	**ta<u>kh</u>t**	board, seat (m) (b
	ن + س + خ =	**nas<u>kh</u>**	Arabic script (m) (c
	ذ + ہ + ن =	**zahan (zehn)**	mind (m) (d
	ج + ذ + ب + ہ =	**jazbah (jazbā)**	emotion (m) (e
	ز + ب + ا + ن =	**zabān**	tongue/ language (f) (f
	ز + ن + د + گ + ی =	**zindagī**	life (f) (g
	ب + ا + ز + ا + ر =	**bāzār**	market (m) (h
	س + ب + ز + ی =	**sabzī**	vegetable (f) (i
	ف + ض + ل =	**fazl**	grace, mercy, (m) (j
	ہ + ف + ت + ہ =	**haftah (haftā)**	week (m) (k
	س + ف + ی + د =	**safed**	white (l

4. Read the following groups of words, focusing on those characters that look similar in form, then write them in Roman script.

درزی	دروازہ	روز	زرد	(a
tailor (m)	*door* (m)	*daily*	*pale*	
				Roman
ذِمہ دار	راز	دُکان دار	مزہ دار	(b
responsible	*secret* (m)	*shopkeeper* (m)	*enjoyable*	
				Roman
خبر	حل	چُست	جلن	(c
news (f)	*solution* (m)	*agile*	*envy* (f)	
				Roman
سجانا	صاحب	بخش	لالچی	(d
to decorate	*sahib* (m)	*giving/granting*	*greedy*	
				Roman

Insight

Remember that six of the vowels are represented at the beginning of a word by ا **alif** and ی **ye** (**ī**, **e**, **ai**), or ا **alif** and و **vāo** (**ū**, **o**, **au**).

اِیکھ	ایک	اَیسا
īkh (*sugarcane*, m)	**ek** (*one*)	**aisā** (*such*)
اُوپر	اولے	اَور
ūpar (*above*)	**ole** (*hailsṭones*, m)	**aur** (*and*)

5. Read the titles of the following films showing at the Jubilee Cinema. Write them in Roman script and then translate them into English.

(a) جُوبلی سِینما کراچی

(b) روزانہ چار شو
بارہ تِین چھ نَو بجے

(c) آخِری سفر

(d) زِندگی اَور مَوت

(e) خبرُدار!

(f) بے اُنصافی

(g) مُنزِل ابھی دُور ہے

(h) جُرُم اَور سزا

The following words appear in the film titles.

QUICK VOCAB

jubilee	جُوبلی	*and*	اَور
cinema (m)	سِنیما	*beware!*	خبرُدار
four	چار	*destination* (f)	مُنزِل
daily	روزانہ	*still*	ابھی
shows (m)	شو	*far*	دُور

twelve	بارہ	*is*	ہے
three	تِین	*injustice* (f)	بے اِنصافی
six	چھ	*crime* (m)	جُرم
nine	نو	*punishment* (f)	سزا
o'clock	بجے	*life* (f)	زِندگی
final	آخِری	*death* (f)	مَوت
journey (m)	سفر		

Answers to practices

1. a) fakhriyah (fakhriyā) b) zakhīm c) farz d) farrukh

2. a) khās b) bukhār c) rukh d) zarā e) mazhab f) lazīz g) zukām h) buzurg i) cīz j) zarūr k) huzūr l) hauz m) fikr n) safar o) sāf

3. a) خبر b) تخت c) تلخ d) ذہن e) جذبہ f) زبان g) زِندگی h) بازار i) سبزی j) فضل k) ہفتہ l) سفید

4. a) zard, roz, darvāzah (darvāzā), darzī b) mazahdār (mazedār), dukāndār, rāz, zimmahdār (zimmedār) c) jalan, cust, hal, khabar d) lālcī, bakhsh, sāhab, sajānā

5. a) jūblī sinemā karācī *Jubilee Cinema Karachi* b) rozānah (rozānā) cār sho, bārah, tīn, cha (chai), nau baje *four shows daily, twelve, three, six, nine o'clock* c) ākhirī safar, '*The Final Journey*' d) zindagī aur maut, '*Life and Death*' e) khabardār!, '*Beware!*' f) beinsāfī, '*Injustice*' g) manzil abhī dūr hai, '*The Destination is Still Far*' h) jurm aur sazah (sazā), '*Crime and Punishment*'

Summary

- The characters ذ zāl, ز ze, and ض zād all represent the same sound (z) for most Urdu speakers.
- The character خ khe completes the series of four characters that have an identical shape to that of ج jīm (ج jīm, چ ce, ح baṛī he, خ khe).
- ذ zāl and ز ze have the same basic shape as د dāl and ر re.
- The basic shape of ف fe is the same as that of ب be.

Unit 9

In this unit three connectors and two non-connectors are introduced. The first three characters were added to the alphabet to represent sounds that occur in Urdu but not in Arabic or Persian.

ٹ	ṭe	connector
ڈ	ḍāl	non-connector
ڑ	ṛe	non-connector
غ	ghain	connector
ق	qāf	connector

Pronunciation

The first three characters represent the retroflex sounds in Urdu. A dot is placed under the letter in the Roman script to distinguish these characters from the dental sounds ت te and د dāl, and the voiced alveolar ر re, introduced in Units 5 and 7. The retroflex sounds are produced by placing the tip of the tongue on the roof of the mouth while the dental sounds are produced by placing the tip of the tongue up against the back of the top teeth. The final two characters in this unit, غ ghain and ق qāf, occur in words that have come into Urdu from Arabic and Persian.

Character	Name	Transliteration	Pronunciation
ٹ	**ṭe**	**ṭ**	the underside of the tip of the tongue touches the roof of the mouth
ڈ	**ḍāl**	**ḍ**	as above but this sound is voiced
ڑ	**ṛe**	**ṛ**	the underside of the tip of the tongue touches the roof of the mouth and, without resting there, is flapped downwards
غ	**<u>gh</u>ain**	**<u>gh</u>**	voiced velar or post-velar fricative, similar to the sound made when gargling; this is the voiced counterpart of خ **<u>kh</u>e**
ق	**qāf**	**q**	a **k** sound made as far back in the throat as possible

Insight

ت **te** and د **dāl** are both pronounced with the tip of the tongue touching the back of the top teeth. The only difference between these sounds is that ت **te** is unvoiced (vocal chords do not vibrate) and د **dāl** is voiced (vocal chords vibrate).

تلنا **talnā** (*to fry*)

دلدل **daldal** (*mire*, f)

ٹ **ṭe** and ڈ **ḍāl** are both pronounced with the tip of the tongue touching the roof of the mouth. Again, the only difference between these sounds is that ٹ **ṭe** is unvoiced (vocal chords do not vibrate) and ڈ **ḍāl** is voiced (the vocal chords vibrate). ڑ **ṛe** is also pronounced with the tongue touching the top of mouth. In the case of ڑ **ṛe**, however, it is flapped down without resting there.

ٹالنا	ڈالنا	لڑکی
ṭālnā (*to put off*)	**ḍālnā** (*to put, pour*)	**laṛkī** (*girl*, f)

Positional forms

The basic shape of ٹ ṭe is the same as that of ب be, پ pe and ت te. There is only one more character (introduced in Unit 10) to complete this series. ڈ ḍāl and ڑ ṛe are part of the same series as د dāl, ذ zāl, ر re and ز ze. On account of its shape, the character ق qāf is conventionally grouped together with the character ف fe although the loop is the same shape as that of ن nūn, whereas the bottom of ف fe is the same as the linear portion of the characters in the ب be series.

Name	Final form (unjoined)	Final form (joined)	Medial form	Initial form	Transliteration
ṭe	ٹ	ـٹ	ـٹـ	ٹـ	ṭ
ḍāl	ڈ	ـڈ	ـڈ	ڈ	ḍ
ṛe	ڑ	ـڑ	ـڑ	ڑ	ṛ[1]
ghain	غ	ـغ	ـغـ	غـ	gh
qāf	ق	ـق	ـقـ	قـ	q

[1]The character ڑ ṛe never occurs at the beginning of a word but this initial form does appear after a non-connector.

Writing practice

Practise drawing the various forms of the characters according to the guidelines given.

ٹ ṭe

For a description of how to draw the four basic shapes of ٹ **ṭe**, see the formation of ب **be** in Unit 1.

ڈ ḍāl

For a description of how to draw the basic shapes of ڈ **ḍāl**, see the formation of د **dāl** in Unit 7.

ڑ ṛe

For a description of how to draw the basic shapes of ڑ **ṛe**, see the formation of ر **re** in Unit 7.

غ ghain

غـ initial form

ـغـ medial form

ـغ final form (joined)

غ final form (unjoined)

ق qāf

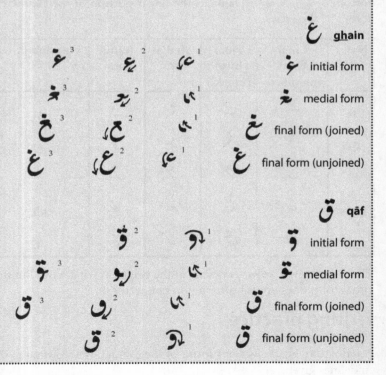

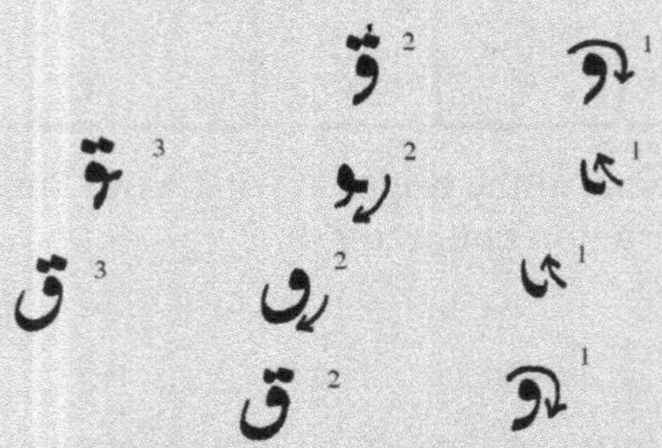

قـ initial form

ـقـ medial form

ـق final form (joined)

ق final form (unjoined)

Reading and writing practice

1. Practise forming the following words according to the directions and then write the Roman equivalents.

Roman	Urdu	Meaning
	1 ٹ 2 ٹ 3 ٹھ 4 ٹھد 5 ٹھند 6 ٹھُنڈ	*cold* (f) (a
	1 ح 2 حق 3 حقو 4 حقو 5 حقوق 6 حُقُوق	*rights* (m) (b
	1 ح 2 حر 3 چر 4 چرا 5 چراع 6 چراغ	*light* (m) (c
	1 ح 2 حغ 3 حغل 4 حغلی 5 چُغلی	*slander* (f) (d
	1 ق 2 قد 3 قد 4 قدی 5 قدیم 6 قدِیم	*ancient* (e
	1 ع 2 عو 3 غو 4 غور	*deep thought* (m) (f

2. Read the following words in Urdu and transliterate them into Roman script.

Meaning	Roman	Urdu
post (f)		ڈاک (a
stamp/ticket (m/f)		ٹِکٹ (b
doctor (m)		ڈاکٹر (c
to read/study		پڑھنا (d
mountain (m)		پہاڑ (e
slave (m)		غُلام (f
Mughal		مُغل (g
chicken (m)		مُرغ (h
able/capable		قابِل (i
time (m)		وقت (j
difference (m)		فرق (k

3. Using the appropriate forms of the characters given, write the following words.

Word	Characters	Roman	Meaning
	ڈ + ی + ڑ + ھ =	**ḍeṛh**	1 1/2 (a
	ح + ق + ی + ق + ت =	**haqīqat**	*reality* (f) (b

	ل + ڑ + ک + ا =	**laṛkā**	*boy* (m) (c
	د + ا + ر + و + غ + ہ =	**dārog͟hah (dārog͟hā)**	*police inspector* (m) (d
	ی + و + ن + ی + و + ر + س + ٹ + ی =	**yūnīvarsiṭī**	*university* (f) (e

Insight

Only eleven of the characters can be aspirated.

بھلا

bhalā (*well-being*, m)

پھل

phal (*fruit*, m)

تھا

thā (*was*)

ٹھیک

ṭhīk (*okay*)

جھیل

jhīl (*lake*, f)

چھ

cha (chai) (*six*)

دھرم

dharm (*religion*, m)

ڈھول

ḍhol (*drum*, m)

پڑھا

paṛhā (*read/studied*)

کھانا

khānā (*food*, m)

گھر

ghar (*home*, m)

4. Read the following phrases, paying close attention to the pronunciation of words that are repeated but for which vowel-markers are provided only the first time the word appears. Note that the order of the words in Urdu is, in most cases, exactly the same as in English, except that they run from right to left.

a (one) small girl	ایک چھوٹی لُڑکی	(a
two intelligent girls	دو ذہِین لُڑکِیاں	(b
the names of three boys	تِین لڑکوں کے نام	(c
four national languages	چار قَومی زبانیں	(d
in five national newspapers	پانچ قومی اخباروں میں	(e
Urdu language	اُردُو زبان	(f
Urdu('s) newspaper	اردو کا اخبار	(g
six local languages	چھ مُقامی زبانیں	(h
seven local people's names	سات مقامی لوگوں کے نام	(i
the washerman's house	دھوبی کا مکان	(j
the colour of the flowers	پھُولوں کا رنگ	(k
the price of eight flowers	آٹھ پھولوں کی قِیمت	(l
nine weeks' time	نَو ہفتوں کا وقت	(m
the cold('s) weather	ٹھنڈ کا مَوسم	(n

5. Read the following advertisement and determine what is being sold. Write out the advertisement in Roman script.

(a اِشتہار (b سَیل سَیل سَیل

(c پُرانی گاڑِیاں (d اچّھی کُوالِٹی بُہت کم قِیمت میں

(e مزدا سُوزُوکی نِسان ٹویوٹا (f دیر مت کرو

advertisement (m)	اِشتہار	*less*	کم
sale (m)	سَیل	*price* (f)	قِیمت
old	پُرانی	*in*	میں
cars (f)	گاڑِیاں	*delay*	دیر
good	اچّھی	*not*	مت
quality (f)	کُوالِٹی	*do*	کرو
very	بُہت		

QUICK VOCAB

Insight

It is hard to aspirate the retroflex flap ڑ **ṛe**. Pay particular attention to the following two common words and try to pronounce ڑ **ṛe** in the second word with a considerable breath.

پڑنا — **paṛnā** (*to lie/fall*)

پڑھنا — **paṛhnā** (*to read/study*)

6. Look up the following timetable and find out where the airline flies in the subcontinent.

(a	سہارا اِنٹرنیشنل			
(b	روانگی	منزِل	روز	وقت
(c	دہلی	کابُل	منگل	صُبح آٹھ بجے
(d	لاہور	کلکتہ	روز	شام سات بجے
(e	کاٹھمانڈُو	کراچی	پیر	شام پانچ بجے
(f	اِسلام آباد	ڈھاکہ	بُدھ	صُبح دس بجے

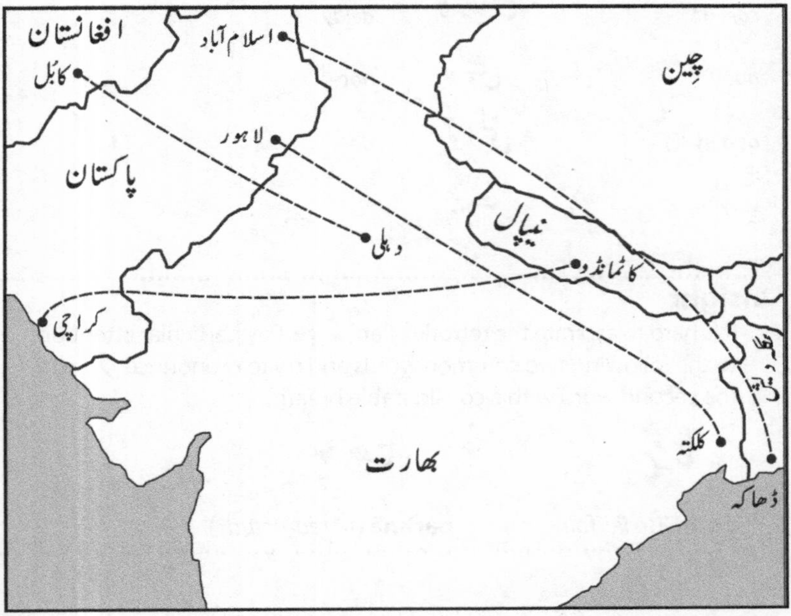

QUICK VOCAB

help/support (m)	سہارا	*daily*	روز
international	اِنٹرنیشنل	*morning* (f)	صُبح
departure (f)	روانگی	*evening* (f)	شام
destination (f)	منزِل	*eight*	آٹھ
day (m)	روز	*seven*	سات
time (m)	وقت	*five*	پانچ
Tuesday (m)	منگل	*ten*	دس
Monday (m)	پیر	*o'clock*	بجے
Wednesday (m)	بدھ		

Answers to practices

1. a) **ṭhanḍ** b) **huqūq** c) **cirāgh** d) **cughlī** e) **qadīm** f) **ghaur**

2. a) **ḍāk** b) **ṭikaṭ** c) **ḍākṭar** d) **paṛhnā** e) **pahāṛ** f) **ghulām** g) **mughal** h) **murgh** i) **qābil** j) **vaqt** k) **farq**

3. a) ڈیڑھ b) حقِیقت c) لڑکا d) داروغہ e) یُونِیورسِٹی

4. a) **ek choṭī laṛkī** b) **do zahīn laṛkiyā̃** c) **tīn laṛkõ ke nām** d) **cār qaumī zabānẽ** e) **pā̃c qaumī akhbārõ mẽ** f) **urdū zabān** g) **urdā kā akhbār** h) **cha (che) muqāmī zabānẽ** i) **sāt muqāmī logõ ke nām** j) **dhobī kā makān** k) **phūlõ kā rang** l) **āṭh phūlõ kī qīmat** m) **nau haftõ kā vaqt** n) **ṭhanḍ kā mausam**

5. a) **ishtahār** *advertisement* b) **sail** *sale* c) **purānī gāṛiyā̃** *old cars* d) **acchī kvāliṭī** *good quality*, **bahut kam qīmat mẽ** *for (in) a low price* e) **mazdā, sūzūkī, nisān, ṭoyoṭā** f) **der mat karo** *don't delay*

6. a) **sahārā inṭarneshanal** *Sahara International* b) **ravāngī manzil roz vaqt** *departure destination day time* c) **dahlī kābul mangal subah āṭh baje** *Delhi Kabul Tuesday morning eight o'clock* d) **lāhaur kalkattah (kalkattā) roz shām sāt baje** *Lahore Calcutta daily evening seven o'clock* e) **kāṭhmānḍū karācī pīr shām pā̃c baje** *Kathmandu Karachi Monday evening five o'clock* f) **islāmābād ḍhākah (ḍhākā) budh subah das baje** *Islamabad Dhaka Wednesday morning ten o'clock*

Summary

- ٹ ṭe, ڈ ḍāl and ڑ ṛe are retroflex sounds in Urdu. Retroflex sounds are produced by placing the tip of the tongue on the roof of the mouth and, in the case of ڑ ṛe, flapping it down as the air escapes.
- غ ghain and ق qāf occur in words that have come into Urdu from Arabic and Persian.
- The sound غ ghain represents is close to that made when gargling.
- ق qāf is similar to the sound **k** but produced as far back in the mouth as possible.

Unit 10

In this unit the final five characters are introduced. They occur in words that have come into Urdu from Arabic and Persian. Four of them are connectors. The first two characters occur rarely in Urdu.

ث	se	connector
ژ	zhe	non-connector
ط	to'e	connector
ظ	zo'e	connector
ع	'ain	connector

Pronunciation

The first four characters represent more or less sounds that are also represented by characters introduced in earlier units. The final character, ع 'ain, however, may represent several sounds and is even silent in certain words.

Character	Name	Transliteration	Pronunciation
ث	se	s	**s** in **s**in
ژ	zhe	z	**z** in plea**s**ure

(*Continued*)

ط	to'e	t	t in ton
ظ	zo'e	z	z in zip
ع	'ain	'	see later in unit

Insight

Now we can see that there are several characters in Urdu that represent the same sounds for most Urdu speakers.

ذ **zāl**	ز **ze**	ض **zād**	ظ **zo'e**	all represent the sound **z**
ث **se**	س **sīn**	ص **svād**		all represent the sound **s**
ت **te**	and	ط **to'e**		represent the dental sound **t**
ہ **choṭī he**	and	ح **baṛī he**		both represent the sound **h** for most speakers in most contexts

Positional forms

Most of the characters introduced here have identical shapes to those of characters that were introduced in earlier units. With the introduction of the character ث se, the ب be series of characters is also now complete (ب be, پ pe, ت te, ٹ ṭe, ث se). ژ zhe has the same shape as ر re, ز ze and ڑ ṛe. Finally, the basic shape of ط to'e and ظ zo'e is the same. As a result, all of these characters are classed together in the alphabet.

Name	Final form (unjoined)	Final form (joined)	Medial form	Initial form	Transliteration
se	ث	ـث	ـثـ	ثـ	**s**
zhe	ژ	ـژ	ـژ	ژ	**z**
to'e	ط	ـط	ـطـ	طـ	**t**
zo'e	ظ	ـظ	ـظـ	ظـ	**z**
'ain	ع	ـع	ـعـ	عـ	**'**

Writing practice

Practise forming these characters according to the guidelines given.

ث **se**

For a description of how to draw the four shapes of ث **se**, see the formation of ب **be** in Unit 1.

ژ **zhe**

For a description of how to draw ژ **zhe**, see the formation of ر **re** in Unit 7.

ط **to'e**

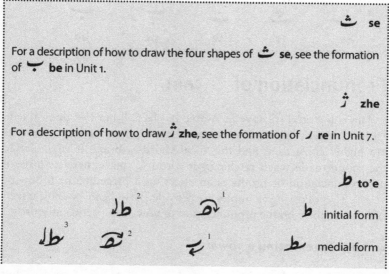

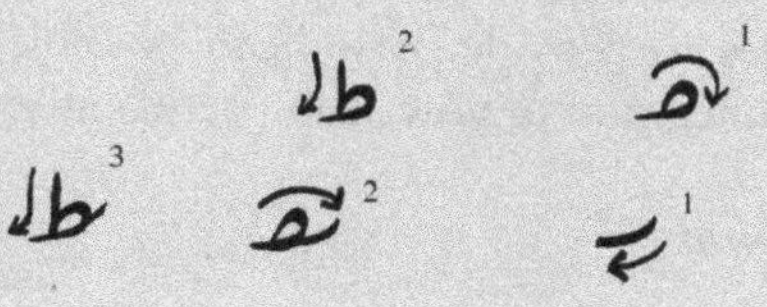

طـ initial form

ـطـ medial form

(*Continued*)

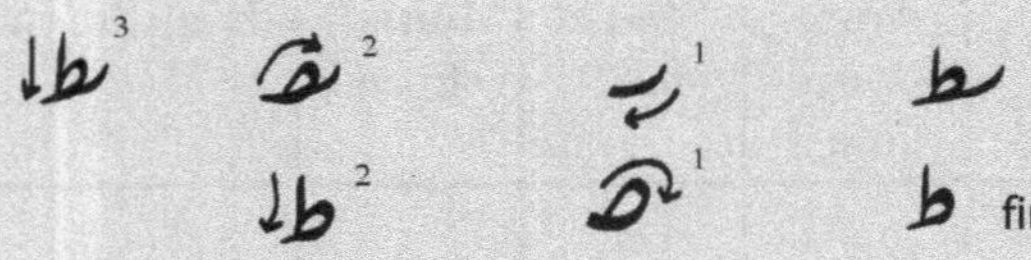

final form (joined)

final form (unjoined)

ظ **zo'e**

For a description of how to draw the four shapes of ظ **zo'e**, see the formation of ط **to'e** just given.

ع **'ain**

For a description of how to draw the four shapes of ع **'ain**, see the formation of غ **ghain** in Unit 9.

Insight

With the introduction of ث **se** in this unit, all of the characters of the ب **be** series have now been introduced. All of them have a similar linear form.

ث	ٹ	ت	پ	ب
se	**ṭe**	**te**	**pe**	**be**

Pronunciation of ع 'ain

ع **'ain** is a glottal fricative in Arabic but has all but lost this value in Urdu. (A glottal fricative is the sound made when the throat muscles are highly constricted and the vocal chords vibrate. It is similar to the sound made when retching.) In Urdu ع **'ain** either has little or no pronunciation or produces an effect on a preceding or following vowel. The following examples are provided to indicate possible effects ع **'ain** can have on the pronunciation of vowels in particular words.

ع 'ain representing a vowel

In many words, ع **'ain** has no real pronunciation of its own but simply indicates the presence of a vowel.

عدالت	عِمارت	عُمر	عیسا
'adālat	**'imārat**	**'umr**	**'īsā**
law court (f)	*building* (f)	*age* (f)	*Jesus*
عَیش	عَورت	عام	دُعا
'aish	**'aurat**	**'ām**	**du'ā**
luxury (m)	*woman* (f)	*ordinary*	*prayer* (f)

ع 'ain influencing the pronunciation of a vowel

In the middle of a word, ع **'ain** may influence a preceding short vowel. This may have the effect of lengthening it. In the following words the Roman transliteration is given first, representing the spelling of the word. This is followed in parentheses by the pronunciation.

استعمال	شعر	معلوُم
isti'māl	**shĕ'r**[1]	**ma'lūm**
(istemāl)	**(sher)**	**(mālūm)**
use (m)	*a couplet (poetry)* (m)	*known*
جعلی	شعلہ	اِعتِبار
ja'lī	**shŏ'lah**[1]	**i'tibār**
(jālī)	**(sholā)**	**(etibār)**
forged	*flame* (m)	*faith* (m)

[1]The symbols above these vowels indicate that they are shorter than the vowels e and o.

جمع	مواقع	توقع
jama'	**mavāqĕ'**	**tavvaqŏ'**
(jamā)	**(mavāqe)**	**(tavvaqo)**
collected	*opportunities* (m)	*hope/expectation* (f)

Silent ع 'ain

In some words ع 'ain is not pronounced. This is often the case when it occurs at the end of a word and follows a long vowel.

مطبُوع
matbū'
(matbū)
agreeable/laudable

ع 'ain as a glottal stop

Occasionally ع 'ain may be pronounced as a glottal stop between two vowels. A glottal stop is the sound that is produced with the release of the glottis (the opening between the vocal chords). This is often lost in Urdu as indicated by the pronunciation in parentheses.

معاف	سعادت
mu'āf	**sa'ādat**
(māf)	**(sādat)**
forgiven	*fortunate*

Reading and writing practice

1. Practise forming the following words according to the guidelines given.

Urdu	Roman	Meaning
1 ط 2 طب 3 طبی 4 طبع 5 طبیع 6 طبیعت	**tabiya't (tabiyat)**	*health, disposition* (f) (a
1 خ 2 خط 3 خطہ 4 خطرہ 5 خطر 6 خطرہ	**<u>kh</u>atrah (<u>kh</u>atrā)**	*danger* (m) (b

1 مـ 2 مصـ 3 مطا 4 مطلـ 5 مطلُب	**matlab**	*meaning* (m)	(c
1 مـ 2 معـ 3 معلـ 4 معلو 5 معلوم 6 معلُوم	**ma'lūm (mālūm)**	*known*	(d

2. Read the following words and transliterate them into Roman script.

Meaning	Roman	Urdu	
capacity (f)		حَیثِیت	(a
debate, argument (f)		بحث	(b
letters (m)		خُطُوط	(c
surface (f)		سطح	(d
apparent		ظاہِر	(e
victorious		مُظّفر	(f

3. Join the appropriate forms of the following characters and write the words listed.

Word	Characters	Roman	Meaning	
	ق + ط + ع + ی =	**qata'ī**	*absolutely*	(a
	ا + ع + ظ + م =	**a'zam (āzam)**	*greatest*	(b
	و + ظ + ی + ف + ہ =	**vazīfah (vazīfā)**	*stipend* (m)	(c

4. Complete the following words by writing in the appropriate number of dots or the symbol that resembles a flat sign above and below characters.

Urdu	Roman	Meaning
ٮحڡٯ	**tahqīq (tehqīq)**	*inquiry* (f) (a
سٮحٮده	**sanjīdah (sanjīdā)**	*serious* (b
ماحوس	**nā<u>kh</u>ush**[2]	*unhappy* (c
رٮڡرٮحرٮسں	**refrījareshan**	*refrigeration* (m) (d
دٮٮل ٮٮکٮٮسں	**ḍenṭal ṭeknishan**	*dental technician* (m) (e
حڡاطٮ	**hifāzat**	*protection* (f) (f
ٮحٮں	**pacpan**	*fifty-five* (g

[2] The pronunciation of this word is exceptional. The character و vāo is written but not really pronounced.

5. Look at the restaurant bill and try to determine what the customers on table four had for dinner. Transliterate these dishes into Roman script.

(a مُحفِل ریسُتوران لاہور

(b دو روغن جوش ____________________

(c ایک چِکن قُورمہ ____________________

(d تِین پالک پِنیر ____________________

(e پانچ نان ____________________

f) چار روٹی	______________________
g) چاول	______________________
h) دال	______________________
i) چھ گُلاب جامُن	______________________

QUICK VOCAB

two	دو	*rice*	چاول
three	تِین	*bread*	نان
four	چار	*roti*	روٹی
five	پانچ	*daal*	دال
six	چھ		

6. What do the following newspaper headlines say? Read them through and then transliterate them into Roman script.

a) روزنامہ جنگ Roman
b) ٹیم کی بیٹنگ کی فِکر نہیں وسیم اکرم Roman
c) لاہور کے عوامی ہسپتال میں آج ہڑتال Roman
d) غرِیبی ہٹانے کی مہم کا اعلان Roman

QUICK VOCAB

daily	روزنامہ	*strike*	ہڑتال
war	جنگ	*poverty*	غربی
team's	ٹیم کی	*removing's*	ہٹانے کی
batting's	بیٹنگ کی	*campaign's* (f)	مہم
worry	فکر	*call* (m)	اعلان
no	نہیں	**kā**	کا
general	عوامی	**ke**	کے
in hospital (m)	ہسپتال میں	**kī** = *'s*	کی
today	آج		

Insight

The word کا **kā** ('s) changes to کی **kī** when the word that follows is feminine.

جان کا مکان   جان کی گاڑی

Jān kā makān (*John's house*, m)   **jān kī gāṛī** (*John's car*, f)

It changes to کے **ke** when the word that follows is masculine plural, or masculine and followed by a postposition.

جان کے دو مکان   جان کے مکان میں

jān ke do makān (*John's two houses*)   **jān ke makān mẽ** (*in John's house*)

Answers to practices

2. a) haisīyat b) bahas (behas) c) <u>kh</u>utūt d) satah (sateh) e) zāhir f) muzaffar

3. a) قطعی b) اَعظم c) وظِیفہ

4. a) تحقیق b) سنجیدہ c) ناخوش d) ریفُرِیجریشن

   e) ڈینٹل ٹیکنِیشن f) حِفاظت g) مچھُن

5. a) mahfil (mehfil) restorān lāhaur, *Mehfil Restaurant, Lahore* b) do ro<u>gh</u>an josh, *two rogan josh* c) ek cikan qormah (qormā), *one chicken korma* d) tīn pālak panīr, *three spinach and cheese dishes* e) pā̃c nān, *five naan* f) cār roṭī, *four rotis* g) cāval, *rice* h) dāl, *daal* i) cha (che) gulāb jāmun, *six gulab jamun*

6. a) roznāmah (roznāmā) jang, *the daily war* b) ṭīm kī baiṭing kī fikr nahī̃ - wasīm akram, *the team's batting (is) not a worry - Wasim Akram* c) lāhaur ke 'avāmī haspatāl mē̃ āj harṭāl, *a strike in the Lahore('s) general hospital today* d) <u>gh</u>arībī haṭāne kī muhim kā a'lān (elān), *poverty removing's campaign's announcement (announcement of a campaign to remove poverty)*

Summary

- The character ث se completes the ب be series (ب be, پ pe, ت te, ٹ ṭe, ث se).
- ژ zhe is grouped with the ر re series of characters (ر re, ز ze, ڑ ṛe, ژ zhe).
- The character ع 'ain either represents a short vowel, is not pronounced or may influence the pronunciation of vowels in a word.

Unit 11

In this unit the symbol ء **hamzā** is introduced as well as exceptional forms of particular characters, the **izāfat** construction, the shortened ا **alif** and the doubling of short vowel-markers. Also included are some notes on exceptional pronunciations.

ء hamzā

ء **hamzā** performs several functions in Urdu, the most important of which is to indicate that one syllable in a word ends in a vowel and the next syllable begins with one. The shape of ء **hamzā** is identical to the top portion of the character ع **'ain** although it also appears in a form which is similar to the Roman letter s.

ء ٔ **hamzā**

If the second syllable begins with a vowel represented by و **vāo**, the ء **hamzā** rests above the ؤ **vāo**. For example:

جاؤ	آؤں	چھوؤ
jāo	**āū̃**	**chūo**
go (imperative)	*shall I come?*	*touch* (imperative)

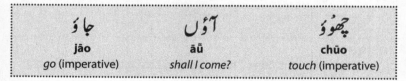

If the second syllable begins with a vowel represented by ی **ye**, ء **hamzā** is said to need a support on which to rest. This support may take several forms depending on the characters that surround ء **hamzā**. For example:

ـئـ	ـئے	ـئی
بھائی	گئے	گئی
bhāī	**gae**	**gaī**
brother (m)	*went* (m pl.)	*went* (f sing.)

There are alternative spellings of some words in which ء **hamzā** occurs. In particular, verbs that end in a consonant to which the ending ئے ie is attached may be encountered with three different spellings. For example:

چاہئے	چاہیے	چاہیئے
cāhie	**cāhie**	**cāhie**
	wanted/needed	

ء **hamzā** is also used to mark the occurrence of two vowels one after the other in a word where the second vowel is not represented by ی **ye** or و **vāo**.

لائق
lāiq
worthy, capable

Insight

If a word contains one of the following characters, it is probably an Arabic, Persian or Turkish word:

خ	ص	ض	غ	ث	ط	ظ	ع
khe	**svād**	**zād**	**ghain**	**se**	**to'e**	**zo'e**	**'ain**

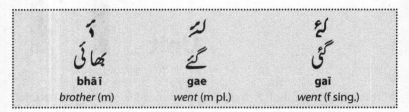

izāfat

izāfat is the name given to a short **e** vowel (pronounced as in the English word **bet**) that is used to mark a relationship between two words. It may be translated into the English *of* as in the phrase, *'the lion of Punjab'*. **izāfat** is represented in the Roman script in this book by the letter **e**. In Urdu it is represented in more than one way.

izāfat represented by ِ zer

In most cases **izāfat** is represented by the vowel symbol ِ **zer**. It is written under the final character of the first word in the phrase.

شیرِ پنجاب

sher-e-panjāb

the lion of Punjab

In many common compounds, ِ zer indicating **izāfat** is not written but is pronounced. For example:

طالبِ علم	or	طالب علم

tālib-e-'ilm

seeker of knowledge (a student) (m)

izāfat represented by ء hamzā

The symbol ء **hamzā** is used to represent **izāfat** when the first word ends in either ہ **choṭī he** or ی **ye**.

قطرۂ آب	ولیٔ کامل
qatrah-e-āb	**valī-e-kāmil**
(qatrā-e-āb)	
(*a*) *drop of water* (m)	*perfect saint* (m)

When izāfat follows a long ā or ū vowel, it is written as ے e, with or without ء hamzā on top.

روئے زمین	صدائے بلند
rū-e-zamīn	**sadā-e-buland**
the surface of the ground (f)	*a high voice* (f)

Modified forms of characters

Several characters in the Urdu alphabet may show slightly modified forms, some of which only do so when they precede or follow particular characters. Two of these, the modified forms of ک kāf گ gāf followed by ا alif or ل lām, were introduced in earlier units. Several more are examined now.

س sīn and ش shīn

The modified form of these characters occurs frequently in Urdu texts. In this form, the initial indented part of the character is replaced by a long sweeping stroke. This alternative form is found both in texts prepared by calligraphers and in ordinary handwritten Urdu. It is found particularly where two of these characters occur consecutively in a word.

پاکستان	سستا	کوشش
pakistān	**sastā**	**koshish**
Pakistan (m)	*cheap*	*endeavour/try* (f)

The indented portion of these characters is also abbreviated in some people's handwriting.

پسند
pasand
liked/chosen

The sweeping strokes of characters such as those in the ب be series and ک kāf and گ gāf are also occasionally extended in the final form according to the space on the page.

Modified characters in the ب be series

Characters in this series (including ی ye and ن nūn) show a slightly modified form when they occur initially or medially and precede characters in the ج jīm series, م mīm and ہ choṭī he.

نو	but	نہیں	بدتر	but	بچانا	تالی	but	تمہارا
nau		**nahī̃**	**badtar**		**bacānā**	**tālī**		**tumhārā**
nine		*no*	*worse*		*to save*	*clapping* (f)		*your*
ہندو	but	پنجرا	لینا	but	پیچھے			
hindū		**pinjarā**	**lenā**		**pīche**			
Hindu		*cage* (m)	*to take*		*behind*			

The same characters are lengthened when they occur in the beginning of a word and are followed by either a character with a rounded form or س sīn or ش shīn.

پسند	تقاضا	بعد	نکلنا
pasand	**taqāzā**	**ba'd (bād)**	**nikalnā**
chosen	*demand* (m)	*after*	*to emerge*

ھ do cashmī he is occasionally found after ل lām, م mīm and ن nūn where ہ choṭī he would be expected.

تمھارا	ھے
tumhārā	**hai**
your	*is/are*

Shortened ا alif

In a few Arabic words a short, detached form of ا **alif** occurs over the final form of ی ye. This is pronounced as a long ā vowel.

اعلیٰ	دعویٰ
a'lā (ālā)	**da'vā (dāvā)**
paramount, highest	*law suit, claim* (m)

Doubled vowel-markers

At the end of particular adverbs that have come from Arabic, the short vowel-markers occur twice. This indicates the presence of a short vowel as well as the consonant **n**. The commonest of these in Urdu involves the vowel symbol َ **zabar**. This indicates a short **a** and is placed over ا **alif**. The vowel, however, is not lengthened.

عادتاً	یقیناً	فوراً	مثلاً
'ādatan	**yaqīnan**	**fauran**	**masalan**
habitually	*certainly*	*immediately*	*for example*

The Arabic definite article ال al

The Arabic definite article ال **al** is found in certain phrases and words that have come into Urdu from Arabic, including people's names and adverbial expressions. It is not always pronounced as it appears. Often the short **a** vowel in **al** is not pronounced and, in its place, the vowel of the preceding word is pronounced. This preceding vowel is shortened if long.

بالکل	فی الحال
bi alkul (bilkul)	**fī alhāl (filhāl)**
absolutely	*at present*

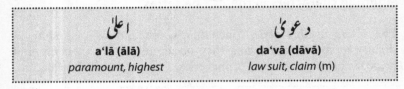

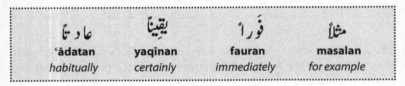

When ال al precedes, one of the following characters, ت te, ث se, د dāl, ذ zāl, ر re, ز ze, س sīn, ش shīn, ص svād, ض zād, ط to'e, ظ zo'e, ل lām or ن nūn, ل lām is not pronounced. In its place the character that follows is pronounced twice. Occasionally the symbol ّ tashdīd is written over this.

السّلام علیکم	و علیکم السّلام
assalām 'alaikum	**va'alaikum assalām (vālaikum assalām)**
a greeting	*the response to this greeting*
(*lit: 'peace be with you'*)	(*lit: 'and peace be with you'*)

Often the short vowel in ال al is pronounced as **u**.

دارالسلطنت	صِراج الدِین
dārussaltanat	**sirājuddīn**
capital (m)	*a name* (*lit: 'lamp of the faith'*)

Further notes on pronunciation

Some words that appear in this book have a pronunciation that does not quite match the Roman transliteration. In such cases the pronunciation has been provided in parentheses. For example, a short a vowel followed by ہ **choṭī he** in a word-final position is often pronounced together as a long ā vowel. For this reason, there exist two spellings of some words in Urdu.

پتہ	or	پتا	کمرہ	or	کمرا
patah (patā)		**patā**	**kamrah (kamrā)**		**kamrā**
address (m)			*room* (m)		

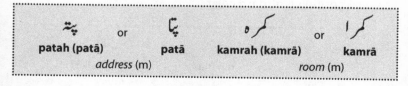

The presence of ہ **choṭī he** or ح **baṛī he** may also influence the pronunciation of a preceding short vowel in other ways. When followed by one of these characters, short **a** and **i** vowels are occasionally pronounced as **e** in the English word **bet** and a short **u** is occasionally pronounced as **o** in the English **go**. This occurs when very little or no vowel sound follows ہ **choṭī he** or ح **baṛī he**. In the following examples, the first form given in Roman represents the transliteration while the second (in parentheses) represents the pronunciation.

پہلا	صحت	مہک
pahlā (pehlā)	**sahat (sehat)**	**mahak (mehak)**
first	*health* (f)	*odour* (f)
مہربانی	محنت	تحفہ
mihrbānī (mehrbānī)	**mihnat (mehnat)**	**tuhfah (tohfā)**
kindness (f)	*labour* (f)	*gift* (m)

However, the pronunciation of a short **a** vowel preceding either ہ **choṭī he** or ح **baṛī he** is not affected in this manner in every word where these conditions apply.For example:

جگہ	وجہ
jagah	**vajah**
place (f)	*reason* (f)

The pronunciation of a few other words in which ہ **choṭī he** occurs in a final position is also irregular.

کہ	نہ	بلکہ
kah (kĕ)	**nah (na)**	**balkah (balkĕ)**
that	*no*	*rather*

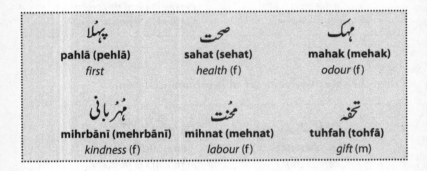

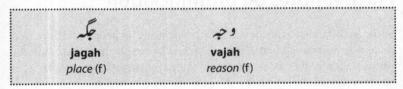

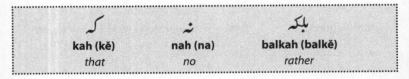

Doubling of ہ choṭī he

In some words both medial and final forms of ہ **choṭī he** occur one after the other. This is done to distinguish words in which the sound **h** is pronounced at the end, from those where it occurs but is pronounced as **ā** or even **ĕ**, such as in the words پتہ **patah** (**patā**), کمرہ **kamrah** (**kamrā**) and کہ **kah** (**kĕ**), etc.

کہہ	سہہ
kahh (keh)	**sahh (seh)**
say	*endure*

Insight

Remember that the indented portion of س **sīn** and ش **shīn** may be replaced by a long sweeping stroke. This often occurs when the next character is also س **sīn** or ش **shīn**.

پاکستان

pākistān (m)
Pakistan

Reading and writing practice

1. Read the following words and then write them in Roman script.

Meaning	Roman	Urdu
for		کے لئے (a
mirror (m)		آئینہ (b
bicycle (f)		سائیکل (c
may go		جائے (d
flight (f)		فلائیٹ (e
save		بچاؤ (f

2. What sort of courses can be studied at the Islamabad Academy? Read the following advertisement and then write the Urdu in Roman script.

Roman	Urdu	
	خواتِین و حضُرات	(a
	بذرِیعہ ڈاک پڑھئے	(b
	اِنگلِش لینگوِج کورس	(c
	اَیئر ہوسٹیس فلائیٹ اِسٹیُوارڈ	(d
	بیُوٹی پارلر کورس	(e
	اَیئر ٹِکٹنگ	(f
	موٹر سائیکل مرمّت	(g
	اِسلام آباد اکیڈمی پوسٹ بکس	(h
	1237 جی پی او اسلام آباد	

QUICK VOCAB

ladies	خواتِین	*by post*	بذرِیعہ ڈاک
and	و	*study* (imperative)	پڑھئے
gentlemen	حضُرات	*repairing* (f)	مرمّت

3. The following is an advertisement for a soft drink that is very popular in India. Transliterate the sentences into Roman script.

(b) نہ کوئی مصنوعی ذائقہ

(c) نہ کوئی کاربونیٹس

(d) نہ بناوٹی مٹھاس

(e) البتہ قُدرتی خُوبیوں سے بھرپور

(f) ۸۵ سال سے ہم سب کا جانا پہچانا

(a) رُوح افزا شربت

(g) ہمدرد

QUICK VOCAB

sherbet (f)	شربت	natural	قُدرتی
no	نہ کوئی	with goodness (f)	خُوبیوں سے
artificial	مصنوعی	for eighty-five years	۸۵ سال سے
flavour (m)	ذائقہ	all of our	ہم سب کا
carbonates	کاربونیٹس	recognized	جانا پہچانا
artificial	بناوٹی	full of	بھرپُور
sweetness (m)	مٹھاس	brand name (m)	رُوح افزا
rather	البتہ		

Answers to practices

1. a) ke liye b) āīnah (āīnā) c) sāīkal d) jāe e) flāīṭ f) bacāo

2. a) khavātīn va hazrāt, *ladies and gentlemen* b) bazariya'h ḍāk (bazariyā) paṛhiye, *study by post* c) inglish laingvīj cors, *English language course* d) aiyar hosṭes flāīṭ isṭyūārḍ, *air hostess flight steward* e) byūṭī pālar cors, *beauty parlour course* f) aiyar ṭikiṭing, *air ticketing* g) moṭar sāīkal marammat, *motorcycle repairing* h) islāmābād akeḍamī posṭ baks, 1237 jī pī o islāmābād *Islamabad Academy post box 1237 GPO Islamabad*

3. a) rūh afzā sharbat (*name of sherbet*) b) nah (nā) koī masnū'ī zāikah (zāikā), *no artificial flavour* c) nah (nā) koī cārboneṭs, *no carbonates* d) nah (nā) banāvaṭī miṭhās, *no artificial sweeteners (sweetness)* e) albattah (albattā) qudratī khūbiyō se bhar pūr, *rather, filled with natural goodness* f) 85 sāl se ham sab kā jānā pahcānā, *for eighty-five years all of our recognized (recognized by us all)* g) hamdard, *brand name*

Summary

- The symbol ء **hamzā** is generally used to mark where one syllable in a word ends in a vowel and the next syllable begins with one.

- **izāfat** is a short **e** vowel which marks a relationship between two words. It is represented either by the vowel marker ِ **zer** or by the final form of ی **ye**, with or without ء **hamzā**. In common compounds it is occasionally omitted in the script but is pronounced. It can be translated by *of* in English.

- Several characters have modified forms, including س **sīn**, ش **shīn** and characters in the ب **be** series.

- ٰ over the character ی **ye** in a final position in some Arabic words gives the pronunciation **ā** in place of **ī**.

- The pronunciation of the Arabic definite article ال **al** depends on the characters that surround it in a word.

- ہ **choṭī he** and ح **baṛī he** often influence the pronunciation of a preceding short **a** vowel.

- Often the pronunciation of a short **a** vowel and ہ **choṭī he** at the end of a word is realized as **ā**.

- In some words in which ہ **choṭī he** is pronounced **h** at the end of a word, its medial and final forms are both written to indicate this.

Appendix

Numbers

1	**ek**	ایک	۱
2	**do**	دو	۲
3	**tīn**	تِین	۳
4	**cār**	چار	۴
5	**pā̃c**	پانچ	۵
6	**cha (chai)**	چھ	۶
7	**sāt**	سات	۷
8	**āṭh**	آٹھ	۸
9	**nau**	نو	۹

10	das	دس	۱۰
11	gyārah	گیارہ	۱۱
12	bārah	بارہ	۱۲
13	terah	تیرہ	۱۳
14	caudah	چودہ	۱۴
15	pandrah	پندرہ	۱۵
16	solah	سولہ	۱۶
17	satrah	سترہ	۱۷
18	aṭṭhārah	اٹھارہ	۱۸
19	unnīs	اُنّیس	۱۹
20	bīs	بیس	۲۰
21	ikkīs	اِکّیس	۲۱
22	bāīs	بائیس	۲۲

23	**teīs**	تیئِس	۲۳
24	**caubīs**	چوبِیس	۲۴
25	**paccīs**	پچّیس	۲۵
26	**chabbīs**	چھبیّس	۲۶
27	**sattāīs**	ستّائِیس	۲۷
28	**aṭṭhāīs**	اٹھائیس	۲۸
29	**untīs**	اُنتِیس	۲۹
30	**tīs**	تِیس	۳۰
31	**ikattīs**	اِکتِیس	۳۱
32	**battīs**	بتِیس	۳۲
33	**taintīs**	تینَتِیس	۳۳
34	**cauntīs**	چونتِیس	۳۴
35	**paintīs**	پیَنتِیس	۳۵

36	**chattīs**	چھتِّیس	۳۶
37	**saintīs**	سَینتِیس	۳۷
38	**aṛtīs**	اڑتِیس	۳۸
39	**untālīs**	اُنتالِیس	۳۹
40	**cālīs**	چالِیس	۴۰
41	**iktālīs**	اِکتالِیس	۴۱
42	**bayālīs**	بیالِیس	۴۲
43	**taintālīs**	تَینتالِیس	۴۳
44	**cavālīs**	چوالِیس	۴۴
45	**paintālīs**	پَینتالِیس	۴۵
46	**chiyālīs**	چھیالِیس	۴۶
47	**saintālīs**	سینتالِیس	۴۷
48	**aṛtālīs**	اڑتالِیس	۴۸

49	**uncās**	اُنچاس	۴۹
50	**pacās**	پچاس	۵۰
51	**ikyāvan**	اِکیاون	۵۱
52	**bāvan**	باون	۵۲
53	**tirpan**	تِرپن	۵۳
54	**cavan**	چون	۵۴
55	**pacpan**	پچپُن	۵۵
56	**chappan**	چھپّن	۵۶
57	**sattāvan**	ستّاون	۵۷
58	**aṭṭhāvan**	اٹھاون	۵۸
59	**unsaṭh**	انُسٹھ	۵۹
60	**sāṭh**	ساٹھ	۶۰
61	**iksaṭh**	اِکسُٹھ	۶۱

62	**bāsaṭh**	باسٹھ	٦٢
63	**tresaṭh**	تریسٹھ	٦٣
64	**caunsaṭh**	چونسٹھ	٦٤
65	**painsaṭh**	پینسٹھ	٦٥
66	**chiyāsaṭh**	چھیاسٹھ	٦٦
67	**saṛsaṭh**	سڑسٹھ	٦٧
68	**aṛsaṭh**	اڑسٹھ	٦٨
69	**unhattar**	اُنہتّر	٦٩
70	**sattar**	ستّر	٧٠
71	**ikhattar**	اِکہتّر	٧١
72	**bahattar**	بہتّر	٧٢
73	**tihattar**	تِہتّر	٧٣
74	**cauhattar**	چَوہتّر	٧٤

75	pichattar	پچھتّر	۷۵
76	chihattar	چھہتّر	۷۶
77	satattar	ستتّر	۷۷
78	aṭhattar	اٹھتّر	۷۸
79	unāssī	اُناسی	۷۹
80	assī	اسّی	۸۰
81	ikāsī	اکاسی	۸۱
82	bayāsī	بیاسی	۸۲
83	tirāsī	تراسی	۸۳
84	caurāsī	چَوراسی	۸۴
85	picāsī	پچاسی	۸۵
86	chiyāsī	چھیاسی	۸۶
87	sattāsī	ستّاسی	۸۷

88	aṭṭhāsī	اٹھاسی	۸۸
89	navāsī	نواسی	۸۹
90	navve	نوّے	۹۰
91	ikānve	اِکانوے	۹۱
92	bānve	بانوے	۹۲
93	tirānve	تِرانوے	۹۳
94	caurānve	چَورانوے	۹۴
95	picānve	پِچانوے	۹۵
96	chiyānve	چھیانوے	۹۶
97	satānve	ستانوے	۹۷
98	aṭṭhānve	اٹھانوے	۹۸
99	nināve	نِنانوے	۹۹

100	**sau**	سَو	١٠٠
101	**ek sau ek**	ایک سَو ایک	١٠١
200	**do sau**	دو سَو	٢٠٠
1,000	**ek hazār**	ایک ہزار	١٠٠٠
10,000	**das hazār**	دس ہزار	١٠،٠٠٠
100,000	**ek lākh**	ایک لاکھ	١،٠٠،٠٠٠
1,000,000	**das lākh**	دس لاکھ	١٠،٠٠،٠٠٠
10,000,000	**ek karoṛ**	ایک کروڑ	١،٠٠،٠٠،٠٠٠
1,000,000,000	**ek arab**	ایک ارب	١،٠٠،٠٠،٠٠،٠٠٠

From 100,000 onwards, commas are placed after two zeros.

Decimals and fractions

۶ **a'shāriyah**	اعشاریّہ **(a'shāriyā)** *decimal point*

For example:

دو ہزار پانچ سو چوبِیس اعشاریّہ دو تِین
۲۵۲۴٫۲۳
do hazār pā̃c sau caubīs a'shāriyā do tīn
two thousand five hundred and twenty-four point two three

0	**sifar**	صِفر
1/4	**ek cauthāī**	ایک چَوتھائی
1/3	**ek tihāī**	ایک تِہائی
1/2	**ādhā**	آدھا
2/3	**do tihāī**	دو تِہائی
3/4	**paun** or **tīn cauthāī**	پَون تِین چَوتھائی
1 1/4	**savā**	سوا
1 1/2	**ḍeṛh**	ڈیڑھ
1 3/4	**paune do**	پَونے دو
2 1/4	**savā do**	سوا دو
2 1/2	**ḍhāī**	ڈھائی
3 1/2	**sāṛhe tīn**	ساڑھے تِین

From 3 1/2 onwards the word ساڑھے sāṛhe precedes the numeral to add one-half. For example:

ساڑھے چار
sāṛhe cār
4 1/2

Dates

Dates are indicated by placing the word سـہ sanh (*year*) without the dot under the numerals together with an abbreviation of the word عیسوی ʿīsvī (*Christian era*). For example:

سـہ ۱۹۴۷ء
1947

Days of the week

پیر **pīr** *Monday*	منگل **mangal** *Tuesday*	بدھ **budh** *Wednesday*	جمعرات **jumʿa rāt (jumerāt)** *Thursday*
جمعہ **jumʿa (jumā)** *Friday*	ہفتہ سنیچر **haftah (haftā)/ sanīcar** *Saturday*	اتوار **itvār** *Sunday*	

Months

Christian calendar

جنوری **janvarī** *January*	فروری **farvarī** *February*	مارچ **mārc** *March*	اپریل **aprail** *April*
مئی **maī** *May*	جون **jūn** *June*	جولائی **jūlāī** *July*	اگست **agast** *August*
ستمبر **sitambar** *September*	اکتوبر **aktūbar** *October*	نومبر **navambar** *November*	دسمبر **disambar** *December*

Muslim calendar

The Muslim calendar dates from 16 July, 622 AD. This is the day after the departure of the prophet Muhammad from Medina to Mecca. Dates according to this calendar are followed by the word ہجری hijrī from the word ہجرہ hījrah (hijrā) which means 'flight'. This is abbreviated with the symbol ھ.

محرّم **muharram**	صفر **safar**	ربیع الاوّل **rabī'ul avval**	ربیع الثانی **rabī'us sānī**
جمادی الاوّل **jumādī ul avval**	جمادی الثانی **jumādī us sānī**	رجب **rajab**	شعبان **sha'bān (shābān)**
رمضان **ramzān**	شوال **shavvāl**	ذی قعدہ **zī qa'dah (zīqād)**	ذی الحجّہ **zī ul hijjah (zulhij)**